Presented To:

_____

From:

_____

Date:

_____

100 WORST EMPLOYEES

OTHER DESTINY IMAGE BOOKS AND MOVIES BY JIM STOVALL

The Ultimate Gift
The Ultimate Life
The Ultimate Journey
The Ultimate Legacy
The Millionaire Map
The Ultimate Financial Plan
Ultimate Hindsight
The Gift of a Legacy
A Christmas Snow
Success Secrets of Super Achievers
Today's the Day!
The Art of Learning and Self-Development
The Art of Productivity
The Art of Presentation
The Art of Communication
The Financial Crossroads
Ultimate Productivity
Keeper of the Flame
The Lamp
Poems, Quotes, and Things to Think About
Wisdom of the Ages
Discovering Joye
Top of the Hill
One Season of Hope
Wisdom for Winners Volume 1, 2, 3, 4

JIM STOVALL & KRISTINE SEXTER

100 WORST EMPLOYEES

LEARNING FROM THE *VERY WORST*
HOW TO BE YOUR VERY BEST

Published and distributed by:
SOUND WISDOM
P.O. Box 310
Shippensburg, PA 17257-0310
717-530-2122
info@soundwisdom.com
www.soundwisdom.com

While efforts have been made to verify information contained in this publication, neither the author nor the publisher assumes any responsibility for errors, inaccuracies, or omissions. While this publication is chock-full of useful, practical information; it is not intended to be legal or accounting advice. All readers are advised to seek competent lawyers and accountants to follow laws and regulations that may apply to specific situations. The reader of this publication assumes responsibility for the use of the information. The author and publisher assume no responsibility or liability whatsoever on the behalf of the reader of this publication.

The scanning, uploading and distribution of this publication via the Internet or via any other means without the permission of the publisher is illegal and punishable by law. Please purchase only authorized editions and do not participate in or encourage piracy of copyrightable materials.

Cover/jacket design by Eileen Rockwell
Interior design by Terry Clifton

ISBN 13 TP: 978-1-64095-114-3
ISBN 13 eBook: 978-1-64095-115-

For Worldwide Distribution, Printed in the U.S.A.
1 2 3 4 5 6 7 8 / 23 22 21 20 19

DEDICATION

The authors dedicate this book to the employees and colleagues we work with who have made this project and everything we do possible. Sometimes all you can do is say, "Thank you."

CONTENTS

INTRODUCTION

BY JIM STOVALL

My Dear Reader,

We are preparing to take a journey together within the pages of this book. As I have written more than forty previous books, eight of which have been turned into movies, I realize you may have journeyed with me many times; or you may be embarking on our first trip together. Like any other trip, it is often made enjoyable as much by who we are traveling with as where we are going.

I consider my coauthor, Kristine Sexter, to be one of the elite human resource experts on the scene today. I met Kristine and got to know her through our mutual involvement in the National Speakers Association. Kristine served as president of our state organization, and I was the beneficiary of much of her talent, wisdom, and hard work. I am proud and fortunate to share this project with her.

Our careers are among the most important elements of our identity here in the 21st century. When you meet a stranger, after you exchange names, it is likely that the next question one of you will ask the other is, "What do you do for a living?" For better or worse, the answer to that question starts filling in the blanks and creating the images that make up who we are. A successful, fulfilling, and positive career can bring us true happiness and contentment in both our professional and our personal life. An unsuccessful career can put us in a place where we feel like an indentured slave—overworked, underpaid, and not appreciated.

As a writer, I have always been a fan of the author Sir Arthur Conan Doyle and his iconic character Sherlock Holmes. One of Holmes' brilliant pieces of wisdom states, "When you have eliminated the impossible, whatever remains, however improbable, must be the truth." I believe we can apply that same insight to our work life and our career. If we explore what the worst employees do and avoid those practices, what remains is excellence.

One of my treasured mentors, the legendary Coach John Wooden, always told his players, "We don't coach effort or attitude, but we are prepared to teach you everything else." I believe if you approach your job with maximum effort and a great attitude while avoiding all of the pitfalls outlined in these pages, you will become a valuable employee and reap all of the rewards that go along with that.

The stories you are about to read are true. Some of the names or places have been altered to protect the guilty. You will find some of the stories to be humorous, while others are shocking or just sad. But all of them are opportunities for you and me to learn, grow, and excel. We have gathered the stories into chapters featuring animal mascots. Our true apologies to any members of the wild kingdom that may be offended by being linked to the worst employees.

When you have read the final page in this book, the initial phase of our trip will have ended, but our journey together will be only beginning. Anytime you have questions, need encouragement, or just want to bounce an idea off someone, I can be reached via jim@jimstovall.com. And you will find Kristine Sexter to be a valuable resource for you or your organization as you contact her at kristine@kristinesexter.com. I want you to know that we are committed to your success and look forward to all the great things that your career has in store for you.

Chapter 1

SLOTH

> Anytime we fail to bring our best efforts to our job, we diminish our employer, our colleagues, and most significantly, ourselves.

Sloths are somewhat cute and adorable creatures that have gotten a bad reputation throughout the centuries. They spend the majority of their time hanging upside down in rain forests and move less than 50 yards each day. This keeps them hidden from predators and works well for their long-term survival, but it does not create any positive images that seem to translate to we humans. Imagine being a sloth and having one of the seven deadly sins named after you. It definitely creates a self-image problem.

When we accept a job, we agree to bring our best efforts, attitudes, and energy to the position. I believe in the adage that tells us the way we do anything is the way we will do everything. You can't be a sloth at work and soar like an eagle in other areas of your life. In the following stories, you will see corrupt and creative ways that sloths in the workplace hurt themselves and everyone in their organization.

Addicted to Social Media

My parents are powerful role models about the value of working hard, saving money and being able to contribute, in a meaningful way, to our community and country. So during the summers when I was 14 and 15 years old, I volunteered at our local hospital in both the cardiac intensive care unit and the children's wing. While I truly enjoyed these opportunities to volunteer and learned a lot about the gift of giving to those facing challenges, I looked forward to the day I would get paid to work! I wanted to make some of my own money so I could occasionally buy something and not have to ask my parents for money. So on the very day I turned 16, I announced that I wanted to spend my birthday putting in applications for part-time jobs.

My first application was the winner! You see, several months back, a family friend, who is a member of a country club, said that she could see me doing very well as an assistant server (aka bus boy) in the food and beverage department.

She was so flattering, saying that I was always so polite, had a warm smile, and a heart for caring for others. She warned me though that they are *very* selective in who they hire—but she would put in a good word for me. After the first job interview of my life (I was so nervous!), it felt great to call my parent's friend and thank her profusely. I got the job!

After a few weeks, I got to know all my coworkers. Nearly everyone was hardworking. They arrived early for work, focused on doing their jobs well, and helped one another when needed. One day, one of my coworkers, a great guy named Darren, disappeared right in the middle of our shift. Darren was known as a really helpful, excellent employee who was well-liked by everyone. At first when we couldn't find him, some of us thought maybe he had gotten sick.

After a quick search of the employee areas, including the bathrooms, we found Darren back on the restaurant floor doing his usual excellent job. "Darren, dude, where did you go? Our supervisor was looking for you. Said he hadn't seen you in the last twenty minutes and it wasn't break time. We tried looking for you so you wouldn't get in trouble. Everything okay?" Darren just shrugged and said, "Yea. Everything's fine. I was here the whole time. Maybe we just missed each other!"

Sadly, Darren quickly became known as "Disappearing Darren." About once every shift, he would simply vanish. Our supervisor became keenly aware of Darren's habit of "going ghost" for about fifteen to twenty minutes every shift he worked.

We found out later, after he was terminated, that Darren simply could not comply with the strict "no cell phone use" policy for his entire six-hour shift. He was sneaking away to update his social media sites apparently unable to resist a "peek and a post" while at work. Now, admittedly, I am an avid social media user as well, but I would never risk this cool job over social media posting.

What a shame that this guy—who was really good at his job and liked by his coworkers and the club members—was too hooked on his phone to simply do his job. I doubt he was LOL about it.

A "Hide-and-Go-Seek Champion"

One of my earliest white-collar jobs in life was being a stock broker albeit trading penny stocks, the ugly scourge of the financial world. I went to work for a company that turned out to be pretty shady and my naïveté allowed me to stay longer than I should have. They sponsored me to pass my Series 7 and sixty-three licenses, which I accomplished on the first attempts unlike many others who failed too often to mention.

On the plus side, they taught me how to make 200 cold calls a day, something I've never seen done anywhere else even among well-seasoned salespeople. I still get compliments for my calling ability as a salesman thirty years later. They also taught me to be incredibly persistent, another trait I have utilized well in my sales career. It was a work-hard, play-hard, testosterone-fueled atmosphere that I really enjoyed in the short time I was there. I developed some great friendships and remain good friends thirty years later with one buddy originally from Philadelphia, who is now a big-shot with a national brokerage firm in Georgia.

It was his and my adventures in sleuthing the where-abouts of the "Hide-and-Go-Seek" champion of our office that I wish to recount.

It seems as if almost every company has an employee who finds a reason *not* to work—birthday party in the office, helping someone with the copy machine, getting twenty drinks of water a day, smoke breaks, coffee breaks, extra-long lunches, eating snacks from the office kitchen, or just asking questions all the time instead of doing his or her job. Our coworker, Eli, displayed quite a few of these bad employee habits.

There is a perfect doppelganger that exists for Eli and that is the cartoon character named Ranger J. Audubon Woodlore, a fussy but crafty and knowledgeable park ranger of Brownstone National Park that appears with Donald Duck of Walt Disney fame in several cartoons. Eli was a rotund, slow moving, soft spoken guy with round spectacles, a boyish face, and a reddish nose. I swear Disney owes Eli money for stealing his likeness, that's how much they resemble each other.

Eli was so out of place in our office and work environment that I could never understand how he worked with this company, especially considering it was commission only. He never made a lot of calls, he didn't really like the phone, and he couldn't close a box if you spotted him three sides down. He wasn't a bad guy, just not the kind of driven individual who fit the mold of success.

Eli loved donuts and anytime they were brought to the office by someone, Eli was first in line, third in line, and usually seventh in line. He really liked to eat. He loved the copy machine and printed useless financial articles all the time to avoid work. He took innumerable coffee breaks and long lunches, but Eli's favorite thing was playing hide-and-go-seek.

In the beginning of our short time working with Eli, my buddy and I would suddenly see Eli disappear and not reappear for thirty minutes at a clip. We knew he didn't smoke, so initially we couldn't figure out where Eli had gone. Did he have a friend in the building he went to talk with? Nah, he really didn't have any friends. Did Eli go outside and take a walk for exercise? Hell no, he never worked up as much as a sweat except when he ran to the front of the donut line. So where was Eli?

One day after trying to see where he went, my buddy snuck out another door and waited outside in the hall to spy on him. When Eli left the office, he was carrying the *Wall Street Journal,* maybe hoping to impress someone because he certainly didn't have any benefit of reading it with his performance. As my buddy tailed him, Eli looked around to see if there was anyone there and then snuck into a stairwell to hide or change floors. As my buddy quietly followed, Eli went to the floor above, a floor with almost no occupancy. When my buddy came out to find Eli, he was gone but just a few feet away was a bathroom. As my buddy entered the bathroom, he saw no one but heard some noise. Suddenly he saw a pair of feet dangling from the toilet. Those were

Eli's shoes. What was even funnier was that my buddy was able to see that Eli took off his pants with suspenders and hung then up on the back of the door. The mystery was now solved.

After my buddy came back to the office and told a small group of us what happened, we began betting every day: how long would Eli spend in the crapper? It was usually a perfect thirty minutes or so. After just a few more weeks, Eli was finally fired and we never saw him again.

The moral of this story is a simple one: employees who spend more of their time finding ways to avoid work are the employees you need to *avoid* as an owner, boss, or coworker. They add no value to your organization and set a poor example.

The Great Cover-Up

I loved cars growing up. Even more so, I loved taking care of cars and keeping them new-looking in spite of the high mileage. So, it was no surprise that my first job at the age of 16 was at a car dealership, cleaning and detailing customer's cars after they were serviced.

Since the wash bay was in the main garage, I got to know all the mechanics and was able to watch each of them perform everything from minor to difficult tasks. It also gave me insight as to the good mechanics versus the not-so-good ones!

One of the not-so-good ones was named Calvin. He was not the youngest or oldest mechanic, but it was fairly clear he was also not one of the better ones. As such, he was usually assigned more mundane maintenance tasks. One such task was to install a roof rack on a customer's brand-new, shiny vehicle. A template was supplied with the rack that indicated where to drill holes in the roof. However, Calvin decided not to use it. He thought he could do it quicker without using the template. Impressively, he was able to speed through it in less than thirty minutes. *Fantastic!* he thought.

Unfortunately, as I pointed out, it was on crooked. "No problem," said Calvin, that's an easy fix. So he moved the rack slightly to the left and re-drilled the new holes. Problem was, there were now two holes in the roof that were exposed. Calvin proceeded to tape over the holes and instructed me to grab some touch-up paint from the parts department. I just knew the customer would see this and be horrified, so I told Calvin he needed to tell the manager he screwed up.

He didn't take my advice and instead drove the car out to be picked up. Eventually it was discovered and Calvin was immediately fired. Apparently this wasn't the first mistake he tried to hide.

Duuuuude!

After six years working my way around in a large company, I was offered a job managing "end-user" computing, which meant I was responsible for the people who purchased, installed, and maintained personal computers and laptops in the company. I was also responsible for the Help Desk where employees could call and get assistance with problems they were having with their equipment or software. There were seven people who worked the Help Desk during a twelve-hour period each day. Soon I promoted one of the Help Desk administrators, as they were known, to supervisor. This was her first time as a supervisor and she took her responsibilities very seriously.

She came to me, after a great deal of analysis, and convinced me that we needed to hire another Help Desk administrator. She followed all the internal HR protocols for posting a job and interviewing internal candidates. Soon she asked me to help her conduct a follow-up interview with one fellow. We agreed to hire "Dude," as I'll call him. She did a great job training him. Soon he was up to speed doing his job.

One day, about three months after Dude had been on the job, she came to tell me that she was getting complaints from the other administrators about Dude. She described the problems—things like slow responses to people requesting assistance, failure to complete his tasks, and general lethargy. I think she was trying to tell me he was a slacker. I gave her some advice about how to coach him and asked her to get back to me in a week to let me know how it was going.

She was back in my office three days later reporting that Dude was napping at his desk. When his coworkers roused him, he was almost incoherent and red-eyed. I asked her if she had any suspicions, and she said she thought drugs were involved. (Now, don't be startled by the rest of the story, this was at least fifteen years ago.)

I made a quick call to HR for some advice. They told me to be ready to transport him along with her to a local industrial medical facility for drug testing. But to first have them both come to my office to confront him with the evidence and find out if there may be some underlying medical condition, but to also ask him about drug use.

So the supervisor and Dude came to my office and the discussion began. Of course, Dude denied any issues at all. After a little pressing through the facts, he did say he'd been at a party the night before where marijuana had been involved, but that he hadn't smoked any but probably inhaled. He was sure that's what was wrong.

So I asked him to accompany us to the medical facility for a drug test. He was extremely reluctant. We all three got in the car and suddenly he was quite talkative admitting to smoking pot in his car during lunch that day—and for several days in a row. We parked in front of the clinic where we discussed the fact that use of illegal drugs was grounds for immediate termination. He made the decision to self-terminate from his job rather than be terminated for cause. Dude was a bright fellow who let drug use affect his work. The lesson for me was to support supervisors when they face employee issues while giving them room to grow in their responsibilities so trust grows in the organization.

Siesta Time

As a long-tenured human resources professional, I thought I had seen it all!

Over the course of several days, I noticed that one of the managers suddenly closed his door at exactly 3 p.m. each day. Because we are an Open Door Policy organization, a closed door is serious. It means that either a manager is coaching an employee or having a conflict-resolution conversation with a peer-level coworker. It seemed odd that this manager's door closed every day, for five days in a row at around 3 p.m. So I gently knocked.

"Joe (not his real name), is everything okay? It's me, Carolyn (not my real name)." I heard a rhythmic noise from within but not a verbal welcome or response came, so I opened the door ever so slightly. Joe was fast asleep and snoring loudly! "Joe! Joe, wake up! The managers' meeting is in three minutes. What's up? Why are you sleeping in your office?"

Joe hastily pulled his legs off his desk and replied, "It's my office. And it's my desk. I can sleep when I want."

Coasting into Retirement

My story is not about one person, or a one-time crazy situation. It is about a "trend" at my company involving people who are nearing retirement.

I work for a well-known energy company that drills for oil. Many of the employees have been with the company twenty, thirty, or even forty years. For some, this is the only place they have ever worked.

Because they have been here for so many decades, they seem to get away with things that others could not. For example, once someone announces they are retiring at the end of the year, those final six months are nothing more than a long social event, and they basically stop working. It starts with them coming to work really late, taking two-hour lunch breaks, and leaving work early. The supervisors and managers seem to just let it happen! If anyone else did this stuff, we'd get fired. The hypocrisy drives me crazy.

Chapter 2

SCORPION

> We win or lose together as a team. Either
> we help everyone on the ship arrive
> safely in port or we will all be lost at sea.

The sight or even the thought of a scorpion strikes fear in the hearts and minds of most people. In reality, the vast majority of scorpions will not attack unless they are first threatened; and in most cases, their venom is not seriously harmful to adult humans. Unfortunately in the workplace, colleagues attack one another for a variety of reasons or no apparent reason at all. From a long-term perspective, it is impossible to elevate ourselves through the process

17

of damaging or diminishing others. My late, great friend and colleague Zig Ziglar was fond of saying, "You can get everything you want out of life if you'll help enough other people get what they want."

If we will approach our work each day with our priorities first set on serving our clients or customers, second on assisting and encouraging our colleagues, and only then think of our own success, we will invariably exceed our wildest expectations. As you read these stories, imagine how different the outcomes would have been had everyone's priorities been adjusted.

All Show and No Dough

In the business world you are taught a lot of valuable lessons along the way, and sadly we sometimes need to make mistakes ourselves to truly learn.

In 1996, I went to work for a very wealthy company that started an Internet company in Asia that sadly failed. Sometimes being right doesn't guarantee success if you are still too early for the market. In my job search, I was introduced to a talented executive from North America who was starting up a new tech company. We arranged a meeting, discussed all the strategies and markets he wanted to grow into, and we agreed to join forces. Along with him and his wife and some developers over in then Yugoslavia, we were off and running.

After all kinds of early success and partnerships with several tech giants, in addition to an intake of venture funding, along with the founder's initial equity, we grew rapidly to multiple international offices and around eighty people at our peak. We participated in fourteen trade shows in twenty-two months across the US, including international locations in Amsterdam, Holland, and Tokyo, Japan. My role grew and grew to where I had many responsibilities, in effect diluting my efforts and focus: painful lesson #1.

One of the tasks I was charged with was hiring an outside sales team. We had representatives throughout the US. It was one of my outside sales hires that taught me the most valuable lesson of my career. Let's just call him "Surfer Dude."

Surfer Dude was the personification of the enviable SoCal surfer guy: well-built, tall, thin, blond, and handsome. He had a ton of confidence but was not annoying about it. His resume was more than enough to justify his hire for us, having successfully worked for major software companies. I really liked him from the first time I met him, and we were complete opposites! Spending a lot of time together during our working relationship, we knew a lot about each other.

After hiring this impressive sales professional, aka Surfer Dude, and several others, we began aggressive sales efforts to grow the company. As time went by, we struggled as the market demand was not as strong as we hoped and we were slightly ahead of our time selling an ASP solution, which is now called SaaS, software as a service.

Reporting to our CEO and COO on a regular basis, they would always inquire about each person's weekly sales success as well as the overall team. Month after month passed and the pressure began to build for greater success. Frustratingly, Surfer Dude, who was seemingly positioned for sales excellence, was faring very poorly. I would have discussions with him on what was needed to do to improve his efforts and his answers initially made sense. But I did not have enough data points to contradict him. The more time went by, it was apparent that I was being deceived. Surfer Dude was more difficult to get on the phone, he had no sales, and his excuses were getting weaker by the moment. Deep down inside I knew what I needed to do, yet I hesitated and waited, not sure what I was hoping for; but hoping for something like revenues suddenly appearing out of the sky when you lead a sales team is really, really bad: painful lesson #2.

As the company kept plodding along with additional tradeshows, great new added partnerships, product improvements and more employees, it was both the best of times and worst of times. When venture capitalists add money to your company, the pressure grows by a magnitude of 100 times at a minimum. Like all great companies, when the pressure is applied at the top, it works its way down and everyone must own their responsibilities, including me as the business development manager. While I delivered a lot of success in many areas, the sales performance was not up to our set-upon goals, and we all know what happens next.

My CEO brought me into the office for a private meeting. During our discussion, I listened intently to all the facts laid out in front of me: "Surfer Dude has the most experience, the biggest resume, and should be selling more than the rest of the team—and he is the worst. You told me you could manage him and yet the results are just not there. On top of that fact, each time we bring him up from SoCal he is tanner and more well-built than the time before. He seems to be hanging out in the sun and going to the gym, but not working hard for us. I refuse to keep paying this guy for no results. Either you fire him or I fire you. Which do you prefer?"

That statement really put things into perspective. I knew my only option was to fire Surfer Dude. My boss said we are going to make the call together—right now! I was nervous as this was the first time I ever fired someone. I called Surfer Dude and reiterated the facts to him and let him know we were parting ways. To say he was shocked would be an understatement. He fought for keeping his job much harder than he ever worked for us. I knew it was the correct decision; and while it bothered me on a personal level, it was long past due.

I'm sure he hates me to this day, but I take some of the blame for allowing it to progress as far as it did. This leads me to my final big painful lesson #3—when you make a mistake in business you *must* address it immediately, own it unconditionally, and fix it as quickly and accurately as possible. I did the exact opposite, thus making it much worse. So my final but most important painful lesson has been learned and remembered forever, making sure I do not repeat that awful mistake.

The Tail Wagging the Dog...or Scorpion

We've always been told growing up that if you do your best, good things will happen. Unfortunately, I learned that's not always the case in the real world.

I was an up-and-coming real estate manager in Dallas, Texas. And commercial real estate was booming! I was with a national property management company that was in charge of one of the largest portfolios of industrial warehouse properties owned by one of the largest insurance companies in the world. I traveled all over the DFW Metroplex making sure their properties were meticulously maintained and tenant satisfaction and retention was high. I even suggested that all of their properties should have similar paint schemes so that each pristine property would quickly be identified as one of theirs. This concept was so well received that the owner adopted it for all of their properties nationwide! Things were going fantastically well.

Two years went by and an opportunity within our company came up that was a great stepping stone for me to get into office building management. I just knew I was a shoo-in for this position and yet I didn't get it. How was this possible? The position was given to another colleague who had less experience and was, at best, just an average property manager.

As I later found out, I was the number one choice for that new position! But the average candidate, the one who ultimately got the position, was heard saying, in his interview, "I am the better choice because you certainly wouldn't want to promote him away from a position in which he excels, do you? He's practically irreplaceable! Just leave him there and give me this new position." And they did. And I left. Who wants to work with employees (actually, at the time, he was still an applicant!) who can convince others to stifle their coworkers careers?!

Two-Faced "Frenemy": Part 1

I worked with Carrie at one of my first jobs after college. We worked at a government entity that was very different from the corporate world. There was no annual review, no culture of accountability, and no motivation to do a great job because raises were all but guaranteed each year (built into the budget).

When I met Carrie, I was fresh out of college with my degree and motivated to learn. I was young and fit and ready to take on the world. Carrie was a little older, jaded, struggled with her weight, and very insecure. She would literally bring in donuts and put two on a plate in front of me, always commenting that I was too skinny. I found this very odd and I was wary of her from the very beginning.

Two-Faced "Frenemy": Part 2

Carrie was also very opinionated. She seemed to take pleasure in looking for a mistake someone made so that she could run and tell the boss, or something that would make her look good. She had her Master's degree and thought she was better than others. She taught me very early in my career that the workplace is not where you find your friends. She was openly self-serving and even managed to ingratiate herself, and eventually become best friends, with the manager of our department. They would take long lunches together, leave early to go shopping, etc. So when our manager started talking to me, in other words simply meaning she got along with me, liked my sense of humor, asked my opinion on things, etc., Carrie felt threatened and began an all-out mission using her weapon of choice to damage my professional reputation and that of all others she felt were threats to her position—gossip mongering!

Carrie would repeat negative comments she overhead. She particularly enjoyed stirring the cauldron of gossip with our manager when she thought it would benefit her in some way. I watched her sow negativity everywhere. She got people fired, spread rumors, and tried to lie her way into a promotion. When our department manager finally left, Carrie was vulnerable without our manager to protect her, and she had to face all the negativity that she had started. It was after I left, but she was eventually fired.

The lessons I learned from Carrie so early on in my HR career still resonate with me today:

- The workplace shouldn't be where you look first to find your friends. When you mix in things like raises, promotions, etc., things can get messy. This is not to be confused with being friendly with your coworkers. By all means, be friendly! Just be very cautious about how personal you choose to get with your coworkers.

- Gossiping will always get you into trouble, so just don't do it. If you have an unhappy coworker, listen (if you want to) but then move on. If all they want to do is complain, watch out. This kind of constant negativity can bring you down too. You never know what may get repeated, and if it's written in an email, remember that those can get forwarded too!

- Being professional for some individuals means that you aren't exactly the same person at work that you are with your friends, and this requires a different mindset while at work. I've witnessed some very talented individuals become frustrated in their careers because of this. They said and did things that were inappropriate in their work environment, and unfortunately their careers suffered because of it. This was sadly what Carrie failed to realize before it was too late—she thrived on the drama in her personal relationships, and did the exact same thing in our workplace!

- Being negative doesn't do anyone any good. Just stop it. Do your best to be positive about your workplace. If you can't, this could be a clear signal that you need to change jobs and find a more positive environment.

- Strive to always be pleasant, diplomatic, and kind. If you want to succeed in business, you must be easy to work with—and above all else, trustworthy!

The Gossiper

I recently heard a consultant speak about the impact gossip is having upon American companies. She went on to list the negative, and measurably detrimental, effect that allowing gossip to occur, and worse, spread, can have on a company. The loss of revenue and thus profit due to the inability to attract and keep great employees because the culture in the workplace can become so unpleasant, almost toxic. And that is what reminded me of the direct experience I had with "The Gossip" (aka T.G.).

At first, T.G. was my "best buddy." Even on my very first day as a commissioned sales representative at a retail store in my local mall, T.G. was warm and welcoming. Always willing to help with my questions, give advice about the products, and even cover for my shift when I was sick and couldn't make it to work.

T.G. also gave me "insights" into what managers to avoid (because they were "jerks") and tidbits of titillating information about all of our other coworkers. For example, one of the other sales reps was always winning the sales goals contests because "He was cavorting with the customers," and how the last sales rep was fired because he was "coming to work drunk" (the truth: he had a traumatic brain injury). This continued for just a short period of time before I quickly realized that T.G. was the classic insecure, jealous coworker.

I quit this job because T.G. was tolerated by management because of T.G.'s excellent sales performance. I really liked that job and I believed in the products, but I could not work with such a flagrant troublemaker and especially for a leadership team that was so hypocritical.

I knew it wouldn't be long before T.G. made up some gossip about me.

C U Latr...I quit

Cellphones are now so ubiquitous that our company has decided to simply "give up" trying to regulate employees' use of them at work.

We did try at one point. About ten years ago, we added some language to our employee handbook that outlined specific guidelines for where and when an employee was permitted to use their own personal cellphone.

Today that policy is about as relevant as keeping a solid inventory of typewriter ribbons in the supply closet. This is especially true as even the executives of the company were routinely breaking the old policy.

Now we have general guidelines and do training on "Personal Device Etiquette" once a year.

But even I was surprised when one of our most respected managers, who was known for her admirable professionalism and communication skills, quit last month. Via text! That's it—no resignation letter, no phone call, not even a two-week notice. Just an early morning text message saying, "I quit. C U latr. Thx."

Update: She apparently packed the bare minimum of her belongings and moved to Hawaii and is enjoying life "off the grid." Solar energy and a water entrapment system in lieu of city utilities. The biggest irony? She does not own a TV, computer, or cell phone.

A Wolf in Sheep's Clothing

As an HR director for an assisted living and long-term memory care company, my experience is that people who work in this industry have big hearts. It is well-known this industry is not high paying. Additionally, caring for senior citizens, many of whom need assistance with their medications, bathing, and other basic daily activities, are relying upon us. They trust us, as do their families who expect that we care for their loved ones with understanding and respect.

One of the resident care assistant's, let's call her Nina, was loved by everyone—the residents, the families, coworkers, and managers. She was always kind and respectful to everyone. She exhibited tremendous patience and understanding when interacting with our residents, several of whom can become easily agitated and become quite difficult to redirect.

One afternoon, Nina approached me to ask if she could speak to me privately. As the HR director, this type of question is common. Nina shared that she had reason to believe that one of her coworkers was stealing money and jewelry from several of the residents. I asked, "What makes you think that?"

"Because two residents said that they couldn't find their ring or watches and another said that forty dollars was missing from her bedside table."

After speaking with the residents, they were indeed missing these items. I then spoke with all staff who had entered the apartments of these residents and asked if they had any insights into these missing items. No one had any knowledge or recollection that was relevant. Protocol requires we contact family members when an incident like this occurs.

Several weeks went by. Sadly, these same two residents reported additional money missing. We followed our protocols and documented our investigation, including contacting the families once again. "I have video footage! I installed a small camera in my mom's apartment after the first incident," shouted one of the family members. He emailed it over to me.

What I saw nearly caused me to faint. It was Nina! When confronted with this evidence, Nina spilled her guts. "I hate her! I knew you would never fire her, so I made it look like she stole from the residents. I have the jewelry and the money. I will return it all to them!"

Nina was referring to another resident care assistant who worked on an opposite shift and with the same residents. She hated this coworker because—are you ready for this?— because her boyfriend said this coworker was hot. What I learned from this was that the old saying, "A wolf in sheep's clothing," is real! Yes. Nina was fired immediately.

Chapter 3

BOAR

> **We will all be known for a lifetime of polite, professional behavior or a few lapses in judgement and decorum.**

As with several of the other animal mascots throughout these chapters, boars or pigs are probably treated unfairly when we think of them as dirty, disgusting, or undesirable creatures. Pigs are actually fairly clean animals and are smarter than most domesticated pets we have around us. I find it fitting that the first story of boar-like behavior involves a limo driver. As a blind person myself, you'll be happy to know that I obviously don't drive a car. When my novels started becoming the basis of major movie projects, I was asked to appear in a cameo role in several of the films. As I wanted to pick a character that wasn't blind, I decided to become the limo driver.

This theme has repeated itself throughout five movies thus far. Not only have I played a limo driver on the big screen, I have employed chauffeurs to drive my own car in the city where I live, and I have hired countless limo drivers to provide transportation when we are on the road. A great limo experience, much like the workplace, is determined more by the quality of the personnel than the surroundings. A cab ride can turn into a limousine experience with a great driver; but conversely, a trip in a brand-new, state-of-the-art, stretch limo can be unpleasant or even disgusting with the wrong driver.

The Bully Shouldn't Drive the Limo

Growing up in a strict, conservative household, our parents always expected my sisters and me to be role models of respect, hard work, and kindness. At times our deference to these principles appeared to work against us, especially when mean-spirited people would notice we were often quick to "give up the fight" in the name of benevolence.

Well, I toed the line on my parent's teachings until the day a coworker went toe-to-toe with me for an opportunity I really coveted.

When I was in college, and just starting to give great thought to a career in law, I worked during the summers and holidays as a limousine driver. Some of the greatest lessons I ever learned I garnered from that job. You had to be dressed impeccably, be renowned for your promptness, have the ability to make polite, yet relevant small talk, and be able to adroitly navigate a 28- foot-long stretch limo in one of this nation's most crowded cities—notorious for its rude and aggressive drivers. Achieving all this was quite a feat for a 19-year-old teenager, but I reveled in the challenge. And it often payed off in great tips!

At the beginning of each shift, the manager would have a meeting to review that day's schedule and any notable upcoming events and driving gigs. Our boss mentioned that in two weeks, a very prominent female politician had contracted with the limo company for a pickup from the airport.

This was an ideal assignment for me! I greatly admired this lady for her work as a public servant and would relish the honor and opportunity of chauffeuring her to her proposed destination. But my coworker, Xavier, also had his own motivations for wanting the chance. The shift manager asked each of us to present our reasons for wanting to do the pickup.

Xavier jumped right in and boasted, "Oh pleeeease! This is a no-brainer, boss! I am one of the most experienced drivers, I have been at this company much longer than him, I'm the most-requested driver in this joint, and I'm definitely better-looking than him!" as he gestured with a crooked thumb at me, while wearing a Cheshire cat-like grin. Xavier continued, "This gal is quite the looker, and they don't call what we do 'a pick-up' for nothin!"

I was undeterred. In my usual polite and respectful tone, I retorted, "I'm unwaveringly responsible, I have a perfect on-time record, I am often complimented for my level of courtesy, and I grew up on the very streets of the city she wishes to go. And my political views match hers. Plus, I can get the security clearance necessary for the transport." The boss gave me the job.

We all knew Xavier was a bully. What we didn't know at the time was that he was also a felon with a warrant out for his arrest. He would never have gotten the security clearance. He quit when the boss found out about him being "on the lamb."

As I dropped my esteemed passenger off at her destination, she gifted me with a compliment that has stuck with me for many years, "From one attorney to a future attorney, I must say that your politeness and respectful demeanor will serve you well. I thoroughly enjoyed my time with you. You are destined for greatness."

The Gum Smacker

For about six years, I worked in a call center. There were more than 100 of us, each in adjoining, little cubicles. I sat next to a woman who was always chewing gum loudly— with her mouth open. Even though we all wore headsets, I could still hear her chomping away, making those gross, saliva-infused sounds. I mustered up the nerve one day to politely ask her to chew with her mouth closed. "Rhonda, I know this might sound weird, but I can hear you chewing your gum. Would you mind closing your mouth when you chew? I'd really appreciate it." She simply said sure, and took her next call. She did well for about two days.

Rhonda actually gnawed on her gum even while on the line with customers. Only after a few customers complained to our supervisor, did Rhonda stop chewing gum while speaking with customers. But instead of throwing her gum away between calls, she stuck it on a piece of cellophane right in front of her, on her desk. When the call ended, she popped that ABC (already been chewed) gum right back in her mouth! Even worse, she would stack the ABC gum up into piles and then reach right back and pop the whole stack back into her mouth. And because the wad was bigger, she made even more noise!

Years later, I still get grossed out when I hear someone chewing with their mouth open.

Pajamas Are Clothes Too

I was working for an interior design firm in a very trendy, hip town on the West Coast. One of the best benefits of that job was the casual-but-chic dress code. Because so many of us were highly creative and proud of our upscale design skills, most of us still dressed to impress but in a fashionable way. Designer jeans with stylish tops and hip shoes was the customary look for all of us, both men and women.

It was a dreary, rainy Monday morning in January. Even for me as a "morning person," it took some stern self-talk to get myself out of bed and dressed (consignment store casual—chic even on the gloomy days!).

As I waited for the elevator in our office building that morning, I noticed out of the corner of my eye, my coworker, Juan. Juan was highly admired for his innovative design skills. Both the managers and the clients praised his vision and creative approaches. The challenge with Juan was his communication skills. Let's just say he was very (very!) difficult to work with. It wasn't that he was the stereotypical "odd creative type." We had lots of those at work, including me. But Juan was just a plain old jerk. Never did a kind or positive word pass his lips to any of his coworkers.

As I look over at Juan, I notice that he is wearing—could it be?!—pajamas!? And with slippers too! He looked like he rolled out of bed, didn't shower, didn't make any effort with his hair. WOW.

"Juan, good morning," I said with a faux lilt in my voice. Another person in the elevator said, "Dude, have they put loft apartments in the building since last week? Did you get lost looking for yours?" A few other folks in the elevator giggled.

Juan's haughty retort was, "I am a highly respected fashion designer and I am starting a new trend for the modern workplace. Pajamas are clothes. And I will be famous for creating a new look." Nearly everyone in the elevator laughed out loud.

Juan did try to come to work in his night clothes for about a week before the boss approached him with hesitation. It turned out that Juan was living two separate lives. Sleep was an afterthought. Between his less-than-pleasant office demeanor and his ridiculous attempt to convince others that pajamas were office wear too, our boss finally realized that even with all of his talent, his lack of focus and absence of a reasonably polite professional presence were too much to continue to put up with. He was let go. Good night, Juan!

Bombs Away

I was born in the early 1960s. I heard my mother often say, "If you use a swear word in my house, I will wash your mouth out with soap!" I never heard a so-to-speak swear word on primetime TV until the late 1990s when the word "a$$" became seemingly accepted during late-night TV, standup comedy shows.

So here we are about 20 percent of the way into the 21st century and it still shocks my system to see and hear the common use of profanity on TV, radio, and, most disturbingly, in the workplace.

We hired a new college grad for our law firm. Within days of his hiring, I was bristling at the frequent, casual use of language that, while not quite the f-bomb level, were still, as of today, only heard on late-night cable stations.

It wasn't long before this new hire did let loose of an f-bomb within hearing distance of a client. This new hire agreed that our firm was not the right place for him.

But I remain disconcerted that the human race is becoming more and more accepting of such gutter-level language.

Jekyll and Hyde

Pretty much everyone I know who has had some experience with interviewing for new hires has a story similar to this one.

The guy interviewed so well. His responses to our stock questions, his references, and his background check were all stellar. So we offered him the job.

About six weeks into the role, I started to hear grumblings that this same guy was making wisecracks and comments about the company, his job, and even the distance from his cubicle to the men's room. I didn't act on this information immediately because I have a policy that I don't react to hearsay or gossip on topics other than those related to our core values, such as safety. But I did open my own eyes and ears a little wider.

About two weeks later, I personally overheard this same guy say to a female coworker, "If you were my wife, I would never let you out of the house wearing that skimpy skirt! It looks way too good on you!"

I reacted immediately. "Excuse me, AJ. Would you please follow me to the conference room? There's a challenge I'd like to discuss with you."

Once seated, his body language, including his red face, showed me he knew he was caught behaving in a manner completely against our core values and policies. Even with that, he took the opportunity to unleash a tirade of all the things he hated about his job. After just two months on the job, I terminated him on the spot. He looked relieved.

Our lesson from this experience: Interviewing is a lot like dating. Everyone puts forth their best in the beginning. We now take the time to conduct more extensive, in-depth interviews, including far-reaching reference checking. We have also trained all employees to come to their manager if there is anything frustrating them or causing them to feel uncomfortable. And lastly, we have enacted a code of conduct and professionalism that clearly outlines that comments such as this person made have no place at our company.

Beyond Being a Curmudgeon

I've been the human resources director of an international company, with 3,000 employees, for more than twenty years. The absolute worst situation I had to deal with was with my own boss. I reported to the CFO, and he was quite the challenge! There is no doubt that he fit the definition of a "toxic employee." No one, even his own boss, the CEO, could deal with him. While his work product was excellent, his horrid communication skills and lack of professionalism was legendary.

For example, he would straight up tell his boss, the CEO, that he thought he was incompetent and needed to go to jail for his mismanagement of the company. He would refuse to attend meetings; and when he did go, was negative and confrontational with everyone. He would grunt as his response to anyone passing him in the hallway and simply saying good morning to him.

But the most awkward part of this was that the CEO would come to me to unload his frustration about this guy!

The CEO was this CFO's boss! He actually asked *me* to talk to him about his demeanor! I actually did try and "manage up" on several occasions whereby I explained to him that he might want to try and be more amenable and pleasant because he might be the reason someone files a hostile work environment lawsuit. He said to me, "Who would do that? You? Go ahead and try it!" And he marched out.

I later found out that the company was in the middle of filing bankruptcy and he was the only one, according the CEO, who knew all of the details.

Chapter 4

ALBATROSS

> **When we don't pull our own weight,
> we drag down everyone else.**

An albatross is an extremely large seabird that hunts by diving into the water to capture fish. They have a wingspan of up to twelve feet making them among the largest birds in the world. Somehow these beautiful creatures have become synonymous with the thought of having a weight around our necks. In an employment situation, regardless of an individual's talent or overall contribution to the organization, there are people who can become an albatross by being annoying or even toxic.

I'm a huge baseball fan and enjoy listening to ballgames throughout the spring and summer each year. There are certain players who have a high batting average, a good homerun record, or perform amazing feats in the field but still become known as being a "cancer in the clubhouse." These are individuals who drag everyone down and become a net negative to the team regardless of their personal performance. Like cancer in our bodies, this is a serious situation that must be treated or removed immediately.

As an employer, I have had the unpleasant duty of firing several people over the years. I have a valued colleague and friend, Beth Sharp, who encouraged me greatly on an occasion when I was faced with firing an employee. Beth said, "You're not firing him, he fired himself." The stories that follow describe situations that simply cannot be allowed to continue.

Let's Not Throw Things at Customers!

Every leader in business must decide what constitutes the difference between poorly chosen behaviors that are merely an opportunity for coaching for correction versus what employee behavior is just outright inexcusable.

For years, when I trained employees, I reinforced the company's expectations to deliver the best customer service. "I want everyone visiting our establishment to have their best customer service experience of the week." Defining this over-the-top customer service means greeting each customer with a smile and welcoming tone of voice. Using a negative tone, cursing at clients, throwing something—even paper—at a client would be considered a firing offense.

So what is good customer service? I remember being in a room with customer service managers employed by Fortune 100 companies, and the question was asked, "Are customer service experts born or made (trained)?" Over 80 percent of customer service professionals said they are born. Then they asked me the same question, "Let me think about it, and we will continue this discussion after the meeting."

One company was very emphatic that they could train *anyone* to be an excellent customer service representative. After thinking about it, I said, "I never hire anyone who I perceive to have bad customer service skills."

Many years ago, I was out of the office and on the phone with an employee who had a customer service issue that was escalating. The client was being insulting, and my employee was not toning down the rhetoric. The next thing I heard was a sharp, sarcastic tone of voice, and the employee throwing something at the client.

Over the years, I have had two hard-fast rules for employees.

One: Don't put a cup with liquid in the trash—pour it out and put the paper in the trash. This shows good housekeeping skills.

Two: Don't park at the front door. This shows your lack of consideration for customers who appreciate having the best parking spaces.

Now I have added a third: Don't throw anything at the customer. This shows your propensity for violence.

I remember visiting with a gentleman at a job fair. He said, "No one will hire me." At first I wanted to dismiss the comment. Then I probed a little. "You see, I threatened my supervisor with violence. The company fired me."

When one has the reputation of being insulting, abusive, offensive, or wounding someone with words or worse, the workplace has a seepage toxicity. If there is a dripping, let it be of pleasantries not behavioral toxins.

You Are Not a Victim

In the early years of my career, I began working for a predominately male-driven local restaurant chain as the manager of human resources. All the hard work, education, and preparation had finally paid off, and I was getting the opportunity I had always dreamed of, or so I thought.

Shortly after joining, the dream began to fade. The reality—I was really hired to clean up their HR messes. For example, the management offices had the culture of a frat house, with parties and games during (yes *during* work!) and after each work day. Working conditions for the restaurant unit managers and staff was subpar, and employees who complained about their working conditions were told, "If you don't like it here, you can leave." One of my coworkers, who held a VP title, was known as the corporate bad boy. He consistently blurred company and personal lines and routinely compromised even basic concepts of workplace professionalism. If you can imagine it, he was probably doing it. He was paid well and he had power.

After several years of trying to educate my peer-level coworkers and others in management, including the owner, on the perils of inappropriate behaviors, it became clear that I was losing the battle. The complaints coming into my office were escalating and I was unable to find any strategy to curb their poor choices. After working long hours and investing a lot of personal time, I was miserable. There was no glory in what I was doing nor was I empowered to change it. I was stressed and hated my job. The office culture was toxic, my boss was a jerk, and I was not in control of changing it.

Over time, messages from my foul-mouthed coworkers echoed in my head. I resented the position I was in and felt powerless to change it. I didn't have an executive coach or a mentor to give me guidance. Until finally one day, it came to me. I needed to take a leap of faith. It was okay to quit. It was painful at the time; but in looking back, it was the right thing to do.

If I could reach back and talk to that young professional I was back then, I would tell her, you are not a victim of your circumstance. You have the power to change your situation. If your values and your aspirations don't line up, then it's not worth doing. In fact, it's okay if you climb the ladder to the top—but if you don't like the view, it's better to start over. You are in charge of the life and the career you make.

You Want the Revenue... or a Smiling Face?

It felt like extortion.

Our top salesperson was generating millions of dollars for our company. Really—millions!

But the irony was that as much as the customers loved him, his coworkers had a completely opposite view.

Customers extolled his "kind, thoughtful, and conscientious demeanor," yet his coworkers were repeatedly reporting to HR that he was "offensive, inappropriate, and dismissive."

It was a very difficult moment for us in HR and in executive roles. Millions of dollars of gross revenue was impressive, and frankly, important. It was our organizational core values that ultimately guided us. We knew that our other employees were watching—and waiting to see if we would choose our principles or the principal.

That was about five years ago. Now we hire to our core values and readily fire those who can't role model our core values. And the revenue? Tripled!

"I Love This Job, But..."

I became a nurse because I love people. I genuinely have a deep compassion for caring for those who are facing health issues. Yet, there is a coworker who drives me crazy complaining about "these patients."

Nurses are in such high demand that I think our hospital is desperate to hire any nurse who shows interest in working here. So when this person started working in our department, we were surprised, even aghast, when the person started saying things like, "I love this job, except for the patients! Haha!"

At first, I chalked it up to light-hearted humor from a new team member who was simply trying to fit in. But after a few months of working with this person, it became clear that this nurse really resented caring for sick and compromised people.

One day I actually asked the person why—why become a nurse if it was such an unhappy career, caring for patients. The response? "Because I knew I'd always have a job."

I'm a Victim of Mall Mentality

Is it me or are some employees always victims or always have an excuse they think justifies their poor work ethic? Seems like no matter where I go in my career (I am in retail), there are always some employees who are always victims.

"I'm late because my boyfriend didn't want me to come to work and leave him alone tonight," or "My mother said that I had to stay home to protect her from her abusive boyfriend," or "My car had two flat tires," or "I use my phone as my alarm clock and I forgot to charge it last night," or "There were three wrecks on the highway getting here." It used to be "My grandmother died," but now it is a litany of convoluted, weak excuses. Maybe its retail or maybe it's because it doesn't pay well. But I am so tired of it.

Not So Indispensable

I work as a welder for a large employer in a small town. Nearly one-third of all residents of the county I live in work for this same employer. The company has a monopoly on the jobs for welders because if you're a welder and you want to live in this town, they are really the only game in town for a job.

Although the job market for welders has always been strong, nearly all of us who are any good can get a job anywhere, but we love this town so we stay with this employer. They offer fair pay and great benefits. The problem is that they need welders so badly that they tolerate a lot of crap from a few specific welders, which they shouldn't.

For example, this one dude, let's call him Will the Welder, would show up late almost every day, would take a two-hour nap in his truck at lunch, and would often disappear toward the end of the day, especially on Fridays. The bosses put up with it because he was the only one who knew how to do a very specialized welding process. He would say, "They can't fire me! I'm the only one around here who knows how to weld that specialized pipe!"

Will the Welder would even threaten to quit if any of the bosses didn't give him what he wanted, like a day off or a raise. Some of us complained and grumbled to HR about how this guy was spreading his negative attitude everywhere and that no one wanted to work with him. I was really angry about how he used his welding skills to extort what he wanted. I was losing respect for the management team pretty fast because they put up with all of this.

About one week after a new plant manager arrived, Will the Wicked Welder went away. The sense of relief of all the workers was real. It didn't take but about a week before a few of us figured out how to do that "specialized weld" that Will said only he knew and used to threaten everyone with.

Things are much better around here now. And we are all cross training to do other things around here so we never have just one person who knows how to do something.

An Open Letter to the Whining Parent

I'm a parent too, but if I have to hear about *your* kid one more time, I'm going to vomit. I know you're frustrated because your kid is a complete hot mess, but you really need to find another sounding board besides your coworkers to aid in your parental therapy. All of us at work are so tired of having to hear the latest chapter of "Poor me, I'm a single parent who is so dedicated to being such a great parent, but my kid is brainwashed against me by my ex."

It takes you over an hour, every day, to weave your woe-is-me story with each individual here, complete with tears. I think it's time to get back to work, because if this continues, your problems get much bigger because you won't have a job!

Sad Personal Situations Affect Us Professionally

I worked with a lovely lady who was so afraid of her husband that she came to work every day super early and left late simply to avoid going home.

While she was not the problem, her husband, and her constant fear of him, caused her to be distracted much of the time at work. We all knew that we were her support system, so we went out of our way to coach her toward positive approaches for improving her life's trajectory.

One day, the husband marched angrily into the lobby of our workplace. Luckily, our receptionist was privy to the situation and acted with great grace and calm. She treated him as she would any client. When he asked to see his wife, she said that she was with a client. She placed him comfortably into a side office, gave him a beverage, and said that she would certainly ensure that his wife would be with him shortly.

I alerted my coworker, the wife, to his arrival. She became very anxious and said that she had filed a restraining order just that morning and was afraid that he was probably there to kill her.

We called the police.

While I know this book is about worst employees, sometimes the worst part is the baggage our fellow employees bring to the workplace with them.

The end of this story? The husband went to jail for charges related to drug procession, and my wonderful coworker divorced him and has moved on.

Chapter 5

LEMMINGS

Following the leader will make you outstanding, while following the herd will make you anonymous.

One of the themes I have repeated consistently throughout a number of my previous books is the idea that we should never take advice from anyone who doesn't have what we want. My formal academic training is in the field of psychology, and among the most amazing theories that has emerged in the last generation is the fact that we become the average of the five people with whom we associate most. Our success, our income, our opinions, our speech, and even our health will move toward the average of these five people. So it is critical that we be intentional regarding the people we spend time with and follow.

A Coup at the Bank

While many of my childhood friends found their first jobs at the mall, fast food restaurants, or cutting lawns, I was able to secure my first job as a bank teller.

This job became possible for me because of the proverbial network—one powerful person calls another powerful person, all in the interest of getting their kids good summer jobs. Essentially, my dad had spent decades in executive leadership at a well-known, financially focused organization. After a few well-placed phone calls, I was hired at a local bank, with branches throughout the state, as a teller.

Frankly, I loved the job and it was well-suited to my strengths. I enjoyed getting to know customers, while at the same time paying strict attention to the details of the role. My drawer always balanced at the end of the day; I was able to ensure all of the protocols were met that are part of deposits, withdrawals, transfers, money orders, and checking transactions.

In short order, I had won two Employee of Month awards and received many compliments from both customers and bank managers alike.

Apparently though, several of my coworkers were not always as happy as I. There was one lady, Eunice, a long-tenured teller, who was well-known for complaining about nearly every aspect of the job—the pay, the benefits, even the awards. She thought I didn't deserve to win Employee of the Month multiple times and that employees should only be allowed to win once, leaving room for others to win even if they didn't meet the requirements of the award.

On a slow morning when most of the bank managers were in a meeting, Eunice gathered all of the tellers into a huddle. She said that she had had enough and that she wanted to form a "Bank Employees Union." In a very calm, maternal-like and convincing tone, she said that all of us "deserved" a raise, better benefits, and better treatment. She said she cared about each one of us as if we were her "own kids," and that all we had to do was to meet with a very nice man—a union representative—sign a few documents, make a small payment for dues and voila, a big raise! She made it sound like a club. Pay your dues, sign and pledge to be loyal, and you were "in like Flynn"! I was asking, "Where do I sign?!"

That night over dinner, my dad asked about my day at work at the bank. I excitedly told him all about this cool new club I was joining at the bank called a union.

The next day, Eunice, me, and one other young worker were transferred to a remote, small branch location. Dad explained that unions were not a negative, but following the words of a coworker and fellow employee without knowing all of the details and points of view of an issue was my error.

I learned to not blindly trust the words of others and to do my research and come to my own conclusion before committing to anything!

Forever 18

I work in the hearing aid business. The most fulfilling part is how we can positively impact the quality of lives of so many who seek our business. I have actually cried when clients are fitted for their hearing aids for the first time. To see their faces light up as they give us a huge smile is so rewarding!

We often hear, "I can't believe how clearly I can hear everything. I wish I had done this sooner! What have I been missing all of these years?" Occasionally, our clients cried too.

We hired Tiffany for the summer. She was the granddaughter of one of our clients and needed some part time work after school let out for the summer. She interviewed very well. Articulate, poised, and mature.

It took only three weeks before Tiffany came to me and said, "I have to pursue my dream. My dream is 'Forever 18.'"

I was confused. "What dream, Tiffany? What are you talking about?"

"Forever 18. You know. The store. In the mall. Hello? You really don't know it?!"

No. Nope. I didn't know about that store then, and I still don't know it now. But I heard that it is a popular clothing store for the teenagers. I hope she has found her dream job.

Chapter 6

CUCKOO BIRD

> We should accept people who are unique, unusual, or even eccentric, but we must reject those who are dangerous or destructive.

While we may not all be big fans of rules, policies, and procedures, there are reasons they exist. There are situations in every career where we must have zero tolerance regarding any deviation from the norm, because the cost of doing anything else is simply too high. If you work in a pizza parlor and you get the order wrong or decide to deviate from the standard recipe, the fix may be as simple as re-doing the order and apologizing to the customer. But if you work in an airline cockpit, atop a skyscraper, or in an operating room, the cost of coloring outside the lines can be life or death.

The "Cowboy Kamikaze"

In the early stages of my working life on the East Coast of the United States, I was a blue-collar guy employed in a great paying union job in the newspaper printing business. I worked with older, tough men who were seasoned by years of dirty, overnight work. It was a job that brought me financial rewards, a lot of fun along the way, and I learned so many lessons—some good and some not so good. I still utilize the good ones today.

What I did learn early on was to pay respect to the machinery, tools, and printing equipment as there was imminent danger if you failed to heed that warning or took things for granted. I became a pupil of one of the bosses who took a liking to me and taught me so much. I was able to take apart and put back together many components of this heavy-duty newspaper printing press.

I left the business in the late 1980s due to the industry's decline, but returned for a short time in the late '90s on the West Coast for an internationally based startup publication. It is here that I met and worked alongside a guy his peers and I nicknamed "The Cowboy Kamikaze."

The Cowboy Kamikaze was sent to work with us journeymen in the pressroom. We learned that he was married and a father of four young children. Within a very short period of time, it become very clear that this young man of twenty-seven was not someone who believed very highly in safety procedures. His work habits were terrible, and he consistently violated safety rules while working as part of a team. I did everything I could to avoid him. We spoke to him in strong language even yelling at him numerous times to stop his risky behavior, but he thought he knew better. The rest of us spoke in negative terms about his work style and shook our heads thinking he would get injured or worse, hurt someone else working with him. Supervisors took appropriate action documenting his foolish misdeeds. He was retrained on the safety protocols and reasons for these procedures.

Less than two months after his start, he decided to go for a motorcycle ride with one of our colleagues at five in the morning, right after our shift ended. The two went out for this ill-fated, early morning motorcycle ride up and down the hills of the Santa Cruz Mountains. Sadly, only one of them returned. The Cowboy Kamikaze apparently rode his motorcycle with the same carelessness and safety-be-damned attitude that he displayed in the pressroom. During the ride, he took off like a speed demon, negligently whipping around curves at 80-90 mph. Tragically, he caught the grill of an 18-wheel tractor trailer coming in the opposite direction and was killed instantly. While we were all saddened the next evening when news was passed to us as to what had happened, no one expressed shock. But everyone felt tremendous sadness for his young family who was left behind.

For me, the moral of this story is a simple one: dangerous and risky people who don't value their own safety, surely won't value yours. Avoid them, and certainly don't follow their lead!

Fake Name

Many people have nicknames or preferred shortened versions of our full names. My cousin's full name is John, but we call him Jack, and my brother's name is Matthew, but he prefers Matt. My friend's name is Penelope, but everyone calls her Penny.

One of the recent hires at my job listed his full birth name on his application and resume as Arthur A. Baum Jr. (not his real full name). Once he started, he asked that the human resources department print his preferred name on his business cards, uniform, and name plate as Adam. Adam Baum.

They refused. He quit the next week.

Flat-Out Mad

I worked for a heavy highway construction company. In essence, we built roads. Some of the equipment used to build roads is massive in size. One of the bigger trucks is called the road roller, which is used to compress asphalt. Some people call it a steam roller even though it certainly does not run on steam.

One Friday afternoon, one of the operators of the road roller was called into HR. He was being terminated.

This guy was so angry about getting fired that as he stormed out of the meeting with HR, he grabbed about six or seven company-owned laptops off of several desks, exited the building, and threw the laptops on the ground. He got back into the road roller and started throwing all kinds of company equipment (small, but very expensive electronics and safety equipment) out the window!

He then proceeded to drive the road roller over the pile of accumulated company belongings. He then punched this huge steam roller into reverse, and rolled back over the stuff again! He rolled forward and backward about four or five times over the stuff before security arrived.

This dude was "steamed" and he started "rolling"!

The company's equipment looked like a pile of dust and trash. And so was that guy's career.

Daiquiri Delivery

One of my direct reports was known for being a "party princess." She actually enjoyed the title and even referred to herself as such. "As the office Party Princess, I strongly suggest we allow alcohol on Friday's after 3 p.m.!" or "Let's all go and do shots at lunch on Mondays. It will make the day go faster!"

One day after working late, I noticed that Party Princess (aka P.P.) was also still at her desk. She was trying to meet the same looming deadline I was. I said, "Don't work too late!"

After getting to my car, I realized that I forgot something. As I got onto the elevator to head back up to the office, a man ran up from behind and said, "Hold the 'vator please." As I held the elevator door open for him, I saw that he was carrying three large Styrofoam cups with limes balanced on top.

As I got off on my floor, he followed me. Right into my office. Miss P.P. came squealing toward him, all big grins and happiness. She hugged him, gave him twenty bucks as she took the three cups from him. Apparently, her favorite bar down the street delivered her favorite cocktails to her.

Evasive Maneuvers

One of my peer-level coworkers never took ownership or credit for any decision or situation. For example, if I were to ask her if she knew why a process had been changed or why a customer account had been switched from someone else to her or even if she was going to participate in the company picnic, all she ever said was, "Go ask my supervisor." Even in emails, any question asked of her was routinely replied with, "Ask my supervisor."

One day I asked her, "Why do you always say, 'Go ask my supervisor' when a question is directed at you?"

Her response? "Go ask my supervisor."

Later on I learned that her supervisor had once told her to direct any question that she didn't have an answer to, to her. She took it as a negative, meaning that she had zero empowerment to make any decision or answer even a simple question.

I think the real reason for the answer was that my coworker was getting back at her supervisor for taking away all of her decision-making power. Sort of a snarky, semi-sarcastic response to feeling chastised.

Avian Aversion

I worked with a guy who was afraid of birds. Our office was on the 22nd floor and the windows didn't really open, so no one knew of his ornithophobia at first. Once when he was in my car, he freaked out when I opened my window to let in the fresh air. He started looking up through the front windshield and out the side window with frantic anxiety, scanning for frightening feathered friends.

I never let the guy in my car again. I avoided him at work too.

Chapter 7

SEAGULL

> **It is amazing how much some people will risk to steal something of very little value.**

As someone who grew up in the middle of the country far from any beaches, I always thought of seagulls as exotic and romantic creatures. Then, on one of my first trips to the ocean as I was eating a bagel with my morning cup of coffee, I discovered to my horror that seagulls are thieves. I realize they don't know they're stealing since we humans are on what they consider to be their beach. I'm sure they simply assume that anything edible is fair game.

On that fateful day, a skilled seagull swooped down and stole the bagel out of my hand without even slowing down or touching one of my fingers. I probably would have admired the gull's talent more if I hadn't lost my bagel.

As we compiled the 100 true stories in this book, it was sad when we realized that there are more stories about theft in the workplace than virtually any other topic. Whatever employees might think they could get away with stealing can't be worth their reputation, their self-esteem, or their career.

Five Finger Discount

For most of my professional life, I have been a professional resume writer. With a penchant for understanding the power that a well-written resume has to positively impact the career (and life) of the job-seeker, I have always found this industry to be both fascinating and richly rewarding. Except when I would catch a thief!

I was working for a nationwide resume writing franchise. During this time as a writer, my regional director recognized my ability to not only produce powerful and compelling resumes, but also for my ability to meet deadlines, be complaint with organizational processes, and train others—especially new hires. After spending eighteen months at one location, I was promoted to regional director overseeing fourteen offices in a multistate territory.

During my very first day as regional director, I walked into one of the offices in my territory, unannounced. My approach was to "mystery shop" each branch office as an ordinary customer. I would then introduce myself as the new regional director and share my feedback with the staff.

As I was waiting to meet with one of the writers, I was able to observe and clearly hear the interactions of one writer with a customer. The writer had no idea that I was there to observe his practices and provide retraining so we could increase revenue at that location. They were concluding the appointment.

The writer said, "How will you pay for services?" The client said, "Do you take cash?" The writer quickly pulled out an off-the-shelf, plain receipt book one might buy from a local office supply store. The use of this blank receipt book was clearly not a company-approved procedure! Based upon company policy he was to use *only* the numbered invoices provided by the company.

Immediately, I knew the operational procedures were not being followed and why. But I also knew I could resolve the matter in the morning.

After the office closed for the day, I used my master key to let myself in. I proceeded to rifle through all of the paperwork including the rogue receipt book. The receipt book was full of under-the-table, cash-paying clients contracting for services.

That evening, I contacted the president of the company to report what happened my first day as a regional director. "You fired him on the spot, didn't you?"

"No, I will go back in the morning and take care of that." As a new regional director, I was not sure how to handle the dismissal. At that point, I knew that I was to have no mercy for writers taking a "five finger discount."

The next morning, I walked into the office and began chatting with the writer. "How many appointments do you have today? Do you have projects in process?" Once I had an understanding of what to expect, I had the conversation.

"I'm not sure resume writing is a good fit for you. By using an off-the-shelf receipt book and not recording your revenue correctly, you need to pursue another job."

"You're firing me. That's not fair."

"May I have your key, please?"

He then walked out and slammed the door.

This is just one of several stories that I can tell about the five finger discount. Apparently there was a cadre of cash hoarders who would post a sign reading, "10% Discount for Cash." They would pocket the cash. Of course they would remove the sign once they heard that a regional director was coming into town, but my "mystery shopper" approach of arriving unannounced put an abrupt end to their scheme.

To borrow a cliché, "Honesty is the best policy."

A Revolting Ruse

I work in a small call center with twelve coworkers. Our job is to take incoming phone calls from customers who have questions or concerns about our products. We work in cubicles, so we can vaguely hear each other.

I was not on the phone when I distinctly heard one of my coworkers start to cry, sob, while on a call. We later learned that this coworker's grandchild had been admitted to a hospital out of state. She couldn't afford the $500 plane ticket to travel to her grandchild's bedside.

Sympathizing, I took up a collection from our coworkers and families so that she could go. This all happened a few days before Christmas, so all of us really had to dig deep to make this happen.

After Christmas, when all of us returned to work, we learned that she never purchased an airplane ticket to go see her ill grandchild. We found out because one of us saw pictures of her on social media during the holidays. In one of the shots, she was caught smiling big, in front of her own Christmas tree, boasting about a brand-new gold bracelet. She had the nerve to take the money and simply stayed home. She admitted that she spent the money on the bracelet.

I seriously could not believe anyone would do this!

She quit the job and is paying us back at the rate of $5 per week. So in two years we might get our money back?!

A Helping Hand with Sticky Fingers

I have worked in the auto repair industry for nearly my entire adult life. I really enjoy the challenges of repairing cars of all types and watching the smiles on the faces of the owners when they pick up their newly repaired car.

A couple of years ago, the owner of the shop hired a new guy. The shop had become very busy and we needed another set of hands. This new guy, however, brought his sticky fingers attached to his helping hands.

It started when I thought I misplaced some small hand tools. We've all experienced it, where you go to look for something and it's not where you typically leave it. So you start thinking, maybe I put it down in a different place or got distracted midway through using it and can't remember where I left it.

After "misplacing" about three of my own small hand tools, I realized that there was no way I lost all three. Most of my tools have been with me since I was a kid. My dad and I used to work on cars when I was a teenager. It was because of him, and all of the great memories I have of working with him on cars, that I became a mechanic in the first place. I treasured those tools because they reminded me of him. Plus, I am known for being organized. My wife teases me that I am more organized than a librarian because my orderliness is better than the Dewey Decimal System!

So I started to ask around to everyone who works at the shop if they had seen my tools. Everyone said no. I went to my boss and explained my dilemma. He said that he would run the security cameras throughout the day, and not just at night to see if any shenanigans were occurring. Only he and I knew that the cameras were rolling during the work day.

It was the new guy. And he was slick, too! Whenever I went to the restroom or lunch, he would casually walk by my work area, and without stopping, pick up a hand tool, put it in his pocket, and keep walking. He would then put it in his truck and take it home.

Only when faced directly with the video evidence did Sticky Fingers admit his crime. He returned all the tools and promptly walked out of the shop and his job. I went on to engrave all of my tools with my name. And the shop owner continued to run the security video live, 24/7. And everyone knew it. Tools no longer disappeared and, interestingly, productivity went up too!

Company Cash at the Casino

I was the human resources manager for a 75-person company located in a city well-known for its gambling and casinos.

Twice a month my department processed payroll. As part of that process, we added additional monies to a salesperson's paycheck if there was an expense report submitted that had signed approval from the person's supervisor.

Our salespersons have company credit cards, and to be reimbursed, they have to have receipts attached to the expense report, and provide documentation as to the reason for the expense. Well, one of our salesperson's expense report showed three cash withdrawals on the company credit card. And all three were from an ATM machine inside a local casino!

As cash withdrawals on a company credit card are strictly prohibited, I approached this salesperson and asked for additional information, insights.

"Oh my gosh! I thought I was using my own card!" Incredulous, I asked, "Three times though?"

"Yea, I guess so," was the response. "I'll pay it all back, right now."

This person did pay the company back, but it was only about three months later when this salesperson quit the job and began attending Gamblers Anonymous meetings.

A Toxic Terror

For about eight years I worked as a welder for a manufacturing company. The company had about 150 workers, and the management team did a pretty good job taking caring of us. Great wages, excellent benefits, and fun stuff like free lunches, employee of the month awards, and a great annual Christmas party.

One year in January, right after the annual bonuses were given, a few weird things started to happen. We would come to work and welding tools would be missing. And then one of the most expensive pieces of equipment in the shop had been vandalized. It looked like someone hit the thing over and over with a ball-peen hammer. The supervisor said that the machine was worth about $100,000 and it was now scrap metal.

Everyone was tense. The managers and the workers were pretty uptight about it. No one wanted to think there was a real jerk among us.

About two weeks later, we found out that the owners had put in video cameras on the shop floor after this happened. Turned out one of the supervisors, who had been with the company over ten years, didn't get the raise and bonus he thought he deserved. Apparently he had been ticked off for a few years over a series of issues that to me, seemed pretty trivial.

The owners pressed charges, and he has to pay for all of the damage he caused. And he obviously lost his job. I was really sad because he has four kids and will probably never find a job as good as the one he had.

A Disappearing Act

I once worked for a residential painting company. My boss was so desperate for workers that they hired practically anyone who applied. It was our job to go into the owner's personal home and prepare the walls, or cabinets, for paint. The prep work actually took longer than the painting part.

There were two separate teams: the prep team and the paint team. I was on the prep team. The prep team had to be a little better at talking to customers because we were the first wave of workers that the customer saw. I learned to make small talk and the customers generally really liked me.

My boss hired a girl who said she really needed a job and would do anything. He put her on my prep team. I was okay with that because she seemed nice, showed up on time every day, and was really good with the customers. One of the customers even tried to recruit her away from the paint company and go to work as a cashier somewhere.

The problem was that this girl would steal stuff. She was slick too! Normally she would disappear to go the bathroom. We are really not supposed to use customers' bathrooms unless we asked. She wouldn't even ask the customer. But that was part of the plan. She would wander around and, if caught, told the customer she was looking for the restroom. In the meantime, she was stealing little things that were lying around: coins, small figurines, even jewelry.

We knew it was her because it started when she was hired and stopped when she was fired. I think she did it for the thrill of it because the stuff she took really wasn't worth much.

It's a Steal

The restaurant industry is ripe with potential opportunities for theft. And as a restaurant manager, I had an employee who was super slick at it.

Twice a day we conduct product inventory using a high-tech tool that reads volumes of product available, especially the stock of beer and alcohol. Combined with security cameras that run 24/7, both inside and outside of the restaurant, there really isn't much opportunity for uncaptured theft. And our employees know that there are "eyes" on all activities.

It took me about a week to figure out what was going on. Premium spirits (the most expensive brands of alcohol) seemed to be selling quite well. Unusually well. I simply thought that the bartender was being effective in upselling the more expensive liquor choices. The reality was that this bartender was indeed upselling but was "split pouring." The drink was poured out of sight of the customer under the edge of the bar on the counter where the sinks are positioned.

This bartender would position two glasses, one meant for the customer's order and the other as a receptacle for the employee to skim for himself. Over the course of the evening, the employee was able to under-pour the customers' drinks, while adding to his own personal stash. He would pour the second glass into a plastic bottle, most often used for juices for cocktails. It equaled about a full bottle of liquor each evening. The employee would then take the juice bottle into the back, placing it into their employee locker.

This theft was not detected by our digital inventory system as the cash register revenues equaled the liquor sold. It was another employee who accidentally noticed what was going on who revealed the theft. The real loser was the customer who was paying for premium liquor but only getting about 75 percent of the pour for which they were paying.

After firing this employee, I thought that if this employee would have put all of these efforts into something legal and ethical, the person would be far more successful. How pathetic.

Dumpster Diving to Catch a Thief

My boss suspected there was a thief among us. She actually figured out how it was happening. And it blew my mind to the extent she went to catch this thief.

There was one employee who was in charge of sweeping floors, cleaning the bathrooms, and putting out the trash each evening after we closed. The trash dumpster was really big. Instead of having a top cover, or lid that was hinged and had to be flipped back to open it, it had a ground level sliding door. We just had to slide open the dumpster door, and throw the trash to the left or right sides of the receptacle, and close the door.

One evening, this employee who was responsible for taking out the trash, got the surprise of his life! He slid the door half-way open, began to break open the plastic trash bags, and remove dozens of brand-new items and toss them into the back seat of his car, which was conveniently parked right next to the dumpster.

What he didn't see, as it was dark, was my manager who was waiting *inside* the dumpster while all of this happened! She was able to video tape all his activity on her phone.

Count Him Out

For years I have worked at an accounting firm as a Senior Accountant and QuickbooksProAdvisor.™ Integrity and attention to detail are, by far, the most critical skills necessary to develop the trust of your clients and thus succeed as an accounting professional.

My coworker was the antithesis of these qualities. For the first several years with the firm, he was a stellar accountant. His accounting skills, combined with his interpersonal skills, were impressive and delightful. Clients praised his work and we, his coworkers, enjoyed his pleasant disposition and ever-present willingness to help anyone of us who asked. This is probably why we didn't see (or want to see?) the slow deterioration of his work and character.

At first he just seemed "not himself" at work. His generous smile became rare and his delightful banter with his coworkers stopped over time. His personal appearance went from being polished and professional to unkempt and disheveled. We just assumed he was going through something in his personal life and simply chose not to speak about it.

We kept quiet until a few clients started to complain to one of the firm's partners. It wasn't long before it came to light that our wonderful coworker had gotten himself into trouble with gambling. His marriage was falling apart. He started to run behind on paying his bills. And that's when he started to bill the clients that he served through our firm, directly. He didn't report his time to us, but created an invoice and had payments directed to him.

We later also discovered he was stealing our software and office supplies on quite a grand scale. Needless to say, he was terminated. I always thought he was lucky the firm didn't prosecute him.

Chapter 8

ALPACA

> Words are all we have to communicate
> our thoughts, our feelings, and our
> dreams. We must use them wisely.

As a college student, I met a very successful local
businessman and he became somewhat of an example,
an advisor, and a mentor to me. Several years later when
I had achieved a certain level of success, we became very
good friends and valued colleagues. One weekend he invited
me to his rural home to check out the new livestock he had

purchased. When I arrived, I discovered that my friend had gone into the alpaca business. When I asked him to tell me about these creatures, he explained, "They are cute, cuddly, and fun, but if you make eye contact with them, they will spit in your face." While this behavior is unpleasant in a large field outside of town, it is unacceptable in the workplace.

Whether our words are written or spoken, they all have a powerful impact. Great carpenters will tell you to "Measure twice and cut once." When dealing with your coworkers, "Think twice then speak once."

Knows I.T. All

I have worked in the Information Technology (IT) field for eight years since graduating from college with a Master's degree in Computer Science and Information Technology. I go to great lengths to make sure I keep my skills current and that I am aware of all the latest changes, improvements, and threats that impact our company's computer system.

Recently, we hired a new IT support specialist. He had just graduated from college and impressed us with his eagerness to help all employees with their computer challenges. But his eagerness soon started to come across as condescending to those he helped. Granted, people's IT skills and computer troubleshooting abilities vary greatly from "expert" to "How do you turn this thing on?" and "How do I use a mouse?" So it is important that a support specialist be patient and able to graciously assist all employees with all levels of knowledge.

I first became aware of the new guy's patronizing manner when he brazenly started telling me how "ridiculously unaware of basic computer operations" several of the folks in accounting were. And that he joked with them about their intelligence level. Since I wasn't his manager, I gently suggested that he might want to simply smile and make all of our internal customers feel well cared for by us.

Well, it didn't take too much longer before the complaints of his Mr. Know It All manner reached our manager. Apparently, he had been heard saying things to fellow employees who requested IT support such as, "Are you serious? You really don't know how to do this?!" and "How can this company entrust you with its finance and accounting if you can't figure out this simple issue with your email?" and "It's okay, I know that your generation is still living in the stone ages before computers were invented."

After that, he didn't last too much longer at the company. I hear he is working for a retail computer store, configuring hardware. In a back room. By himself. And he loves it.

The 1-Day Employee

Being the owners of a very small company, every decision to hire someone either as a contractor or employee is a big deal. We had spent months considering adding someone to focus on sales and marketing and were on the hunt for just the right person to work alongside us. Our search involved word-of-mouth as well as considering people we knew.

One day, we received a call from a young man whom we had known as a teenager. We had lost track of him over the years, so it was good to hear from him. We all got together for lunch just to catch up and learned that "Dan," as I'll call him, had been in marketing and sales for a few different companies and seemed to have a heart for that type of work. He was looking for something new that would offer him flexibility and required very little travel. While our lunch meeting was intended primarily to catch up on life, we thought perhaps Dan might be a fit.

A few weeks later, we asked Dan if we could talk with him about an opportunity in our company. We both met with him together and individually over a period of a few days to see if he was a good fit and if he was interested in the work. He expressed great interest in working with us because he liked what we do and we shared similar values.

We all came to the decision that this was going to be a great match and decided to move forward with an offer. He said he wanted to discuss this with his wife and make sure it was the right decision. Of course, no problem! He called late that afternoon and told us how excited he was and eager to start the following Monday—just four days away.

We got busy making office arrangements and ordered a new laptop within a few hours. We had also discussed his participation in a conference later that month recognizing that he didn't want to travel much but was willing to be on the road a few days each quarter. We made those travel arrangements and registered him for the conference. No time wasted there!

The next morning, I sent Dan an email with all of the information about his office arrangements as well as his travel information for the conference, which he had been excited about attending in San Diego. I didn't get a reply. I waited several hours and then called Dan to see if he had received the information.

There was silence on the line.

Then Dan said, "Didn't you get the voice mail I left this morning that said I decided I didn't want to take the job?"

Lesson learned: take time for onboarding before moving too fast, especially in a small company.

Social Media Reveals the Real Person

It is amazing how brazen people become when they hide behind their keyboard.

I once worked with a person who, while at work, was a pleasant, professional, and gracious coworker. I enjoyed working with this individual and had no reason to think that we had any negative issues between us.

Then I began receiving scathing emails from someone I didn't know. These emails would come to my work email box. The sender hid behind a generic email name, using a free email source (similar to Gmail or Yahoo mail). The content of the emails was pretty vicious. The sender would criticize my political and religious views, call me names ("Fancy Fat Butt"), and make really derogatory suggestions such as, "You really need to do something about your hair—it's so ugly."

Because the emails were coming only to my work email box, I reported them to the IT director. Well, it didn't take long for the IT department to track down the sender. It was the coworker who I thought was so pleasant and professional!

When confronted with the evidence from IT, this person said, "I know it was wrong to send these emails, but I couldn't help myself from expressing how wrong I think their religious views, political choices, and personal grooming are! I wanted to influence this person to make a different choice of faith, political party, and hairstyle. That's all. I just wanted to help!"

This person was terminated that day.

Chapter 9

CATERPILLARS AND BUTTERFLIES

> **Regardless of conditions once upon a time, we can be successful and live happily ever after.**

Nature offers us many miracles all around us every day. Among the most dramatic of these miracles is the metamorphosis of a caterpillar into a butterfly. This dramatic change can become a reality in our personal and professional lives. We must remember that our past as well as our present does not command our future. The most influential book in the field of success and personal development is Napoleon Hill's landmark literary achievement entitled, *Think and Grow Rich*. Although this book is over 70 years old, it remains among the top-selling titles, having sold over 100 million copies worldwide. Among the many foundational truths in *Think and Grow Rich* is the principle that every adversity is endowed with the seed of a greater good. Opportunities often come disguised as problems. This is certainly true in the workplace.

The whole world is praying for a great idea, and they trip over one several times each week. All that you need to do to have a great idea is to go through your daily routine on the job and wait for something bad to happen, then ask yourself the magic question, "How could I have avoided that?" The answer to that question is a great idea. The only thing you need to do to turn your great idea into a business opportunity or breakthrough for your organization is to ask one further question, "How can I help other people avoid that problem?" Once you understand this principle, you will begin to look at problems, challenges, and the worst employees in a new way.

When Sparks Fly

After spending 53 years as a licensed electrician, I retired at 77 years old. During the first few months of retirement, I relished sleeping in until the very late hour of 7 a.m. (most work mornings started at 4:30 a.m.), being relieved of the stress of deadlines and project completion dates, and being able to pursue my hobby of reading historical biographies at any time of any day.

After about six months of this eagerly anticipated retirement, I realized I was getting really bored. Plus my wife said I was getting on her nerves and that I "better get my a$$ out of the damn chair, get out of the house, and do something productive."

So I decided to do what I know best. I made a plan to rewire the whole house! I live in an older home, and the electrical systems were outdated by current standards. (Pun intended, "current," get it!?) For years I had planned to bring all of the wiring up to present-day electrical code. So I headed off to the nearby big-box hardware store.

As I was wandering the wonderfully stocked electrical aisle jam-packed with every ballast, conduit, voltage meter, switch, fitting, and breakers, I realized how much I missed the world of electrical work. Perusing these aisles was like visiting a toy store or spending time with familiar friends. I was happy and feeling purposeful again. And I knew the wife would stop nagging, I mean requesting, that I "do something" around the house. Perfect!

Over the course of the next month, I probably went to that hardware store and strolled my favorite aisle of electrical supplies more than twenty times. On several occasions, I was able to help other fellow shoppers who were obviously unsure of what parts they needed for a DIY project. The telltale signs of electrical parts confusion: deer-in-the-headlights look, pacing up and down the aisles, trying to read the small print on the shelf labels or audible outbursts such as, "Why is there never anyone to help us in these aisles?"

On my next visit to the store, a guy wearing a manager nametag politely smiled at me as he walked by. Suddenly, he did an about-face and said, "I notice that you are here a lot. Are you a contractor? Have you signed up for our discount for contractors and businesses?"

"Nah, I'm a retired electrician and just working on a small home project." He cocked his head to the side as if he had a sudden, bright idea, like a light bulb came on. (Pun intended again, "lightbulb moment.")

"How about a job here? We have been short-handed in the electrical department for some time now. And ya know, I think I have heard about you from a customer who wanted to compliment our employee who helped him in the electrical department. But I knew we didn't have an employee in this department. That must have been you!"

"Yes, it probably was me as I have helped quite a few of your customers. But it was my pleasure to help."

He then replied, "You'll get a discount if you work here! And all you have to do is work ten hours a week minimum. I can hire you today!"

That day I went home not just with a few more electrical parts, but a job too! The wife was really happy.

Everything was great until I had to work with another employee named Joe. Joe was a jerk, plain and simple. He never smiled, grunted and grumbled at coworkers and customers alike. He was openly hostile to me, saying things like, "Hey Sparky, aren't you a little old to be working at a minimum wage job?" or "You're the store manager's favorite. He's always giving you all the easy hours leaving me with the lame hours." Joe's antics got to the point whereby I was ready to quit. I didn't need this type of poor behavior from a coworker at this point in my life. But I stayed on because it was November, and they really needed the help during the holidays.

On a cold, icy morning, I walked into work, headed for the employee locker room to put away my coat. Joe followed me in and spouted off another sarcastic comment. As I tried to finally tell Joe to can it and zip it, a searing pain ripped across my chest. I went down to the ground hugging my chest unable to breathe.

Joe reacted with swift confidence. He seemed to recognize what was happening to me. Without hesitation, Joe shouted for a coworker to call 911. And that was all I remembered.

I woke up in the hospital. At my bedside were my wife, my boss, and Joe. "What happened?" I asked. My wife responded, "You had a heart attack at work. You stopped breathing and your heart stopped. Joe knew how to use the defibrillator that was hanging right there in the employee breakroom. Joe saved your life!"

Joe changed after that day. He became one of the most helpful, kind, and nicest coworkers I have ever known. The reason he said that he was so difficult to deal with and unhappy was that he had just lost his father to a heart attack. No one who was with his father at the time knew how to help, and subsequently, he died. He was taking out his anger on everyone around him both at home and at work. But Joe had made the decision to take CPR lessons and learn to use a defibrillator just one week before my heart attack at work.

I changed too. I let Joe call me Sparky now. It seems only fitting that a device that uses electrical current, wielded by Joe, is what saved my life.

Joe went from being the worst employee, to the best.

The Hot Potato Employee

After seventeen years in the private sector as a manager for a Fortune 100 company, I followed my passion and took a leadership position serving at-risk youth and children with a state governmental agency.

I looked forward to working with like-minded, kind-hearted coworkers who all rallied together to serve these kids.

Within the month of arriving at this new role, I was informed that I was being assigned a team of three employees to supervise. As an experienced manager of high functioning teams, I warmly welcomed this opportunity.

Each of these three employees had varying degrees of tenure and possessed different skill sets. Two of the employees were outstanding in their roles: committed to the vision and mission of the organization and delivered impressive outcomes with their kids. The third employee who, incidentally, had been at the organization the longest (thirteen years), was openly hostile with other coworkers ("I am NOT going to work with him. He's a brownnose and the favorite of the executive director"). Additionally, this employee was consistently argumentative and late to work and meetings on a daily basis.

I learned that this employee was actually known as "The Hot Potato." Passed from manager to manager over the years, stories of the noncooperative, passive aggressive behaviors of this person were legendary.

I devised a plan. It was actually quite simple. I decided to use the communication skills and trust-building approaches we all utilize when working with the youth we serve.

After much active listening, I learned that this employee lost trust in an immediate supervisor many years ago when promised an opportunity to develop a new program. When the program was a huge success, the supervisor took credit for it never crediting this employee for it.

Once I assured this employee that I lead from a foundation of servant leadership, whereby I see my role as being responsible for ensuring the continued success of those who report to me, this employee began to excel.

The Hugger

I get it, some people are huggers and some are not. At my job in a regional health center, we had one employee who, when seeing those she had not seen in some time, would hug them. Admittedly, when others would extend their hand, presumably to shake hands as a greeting, she would grab their open hand and pull them in. "I'm a hugger," she would exclaim.

The problem was she would stay in a closely clasped, full body hug, for an awkward, lengthy amount of time.

Occasionally she would make what she called "yummy noises," similar to a moan, to communicate how delightful it was to hug that person.

One day, she wore a shirt to work that said, "Free Hugs." She said that our society was becoming too aloof, detached and unfriendly, and that the human touch had healing powers; and as healthcare professionals, it was our job to demonstrate that hugs were medicinal.

One day she didn't show up to work. Apparently, a patient's wife found out that her hugs were causing heart palpitations for her critically ill husband.

We heard that she now works for the zoo and has a genuine title as a "Snuggler" for baby mammals. She says she loves her job, and her job loves her.

The lesson is that we all have different definitions of personal space. And that we must respect those differences.

Going to the Dogs or Rather Dogs "Going..."

As a state agency, we have offices in nearly every county. Most of these offices have just two or three employees each. As the senior manager, I travel the state spending time in each office. So with twenty-six counties, I visit each office only once every month or so.

One of our county offices was located in a beautifully appointed 100-year-old building. The building was on the National Register of Historical Places: marble columns, intricate wood inlays on the walls, fresco paintings on the ceilings, and stunningly beautiful parquet wood floors. This branch office was definitely envied by many of our employees, most of whom worked in 1970s or '80s government-style office buildings, all in great need of updating.

While most of the time my employees know exactly when I'm coming, I decided to arrive, unannounced, to each of the branch offices this month.

Upon arriving at the beautiful historical office, I stopped to, once again, admire the beauty of this building. Even the flowers and landscaping were simply magnificent.

I walked the one flight of marble stairs to the main door to our office. The instant I turned the knob and entered, it hit me. The stench. About three seconds later, I was literally charged by a pack of…puppies.

The smell was a result of the dozen puppy wee-wee training pads spread all over the floor.

I called out to my branch manager, "Shanice! Shanice, are you here?" I tiptoed on the drier looking edges of the wee-wee pads on the floor in search of my staff member. The dogs went with me, encircling my ankles. I called out to the second staff member assigned to this office, "Ryan! Is anyone here?"

A minute later, both employees emerged from the break room, looking shocked to see me. "Oh Linda, we didn't know you were coming today! I am so sorry about the dogs. I know it looks bad, but…"

I cut her off, "It looks bad, but it smells worse! What the heck is happening here?"

"My dog had puppies and I didn't have the heart to leave them at home all day. I promise, it's only been a few weeks..."

"Weeks?! Weeks? You've had these dogs urinating and defecating all over the floors of a state agency office for weeks?" I was incredulous.

The state agency had to pay to replace the 100-year-old, nearly irreplaceable floors. We were evicted (yes, a state agency was evicted) from the most beautiful office building so many of us admired. Shanice was reprimanded and now works in our new location: a very, very ugly 1975, one story commercial retail space. But the best part—I adopted one of the puppies!

From Meanie to Meaningful

As a healthcare professional, I see my role as twofold: clinician and listener. As a clinician, I have to understand the scientific, technical, and physiological aspects of caring for people. Much of that knowledge comes from medical school, day-to-day experience, and ongoing academic study. But nowhere in medical school, or even from a textbook, are we taught how to be effective listeners.

Thankfully, most people who enter the healthcare field bring a natural affinity for compassion and the ability to simply listen to what our patients and their families tell us. But occasionally a real curmudgeon can be found among us!

Dr. A was simply a jerk. While he had a brilliant, scientific mind and could diagnose the rarest, most obscure maladies in moments, his verbal communication skills could only be deemed horrid at best. He would routinely interrupt, tell patients and colleagues that they were "flat-out wrong," and even walk away from others mid-sentence. Atrocious bedside manner!

One evening, a few intensive care unit nurses pulled me aside and told me that Dr. A did something that changed everyone's mind about him. He was caring for a very elderly man who was receiving hospice care as it was quite apparent that this gentleman would probably not live through the night. The nurses shared that this patient was himself a physician and sadly, he had no family whatsoever.

Without saying a word to anyone, Dr. A sat at the bedside of this fellow physician gently holding his hand for the final hours, and breaths, of this lonely man.

Many fellow healthcare professionals, upon hearing about Dr. A's tender heart, became a little more forgiving of his abrupt persona.

Loud Mouth

For five years I worked in a call center for one of the country's largest retailers. We sat in cubicles, arranged by department, in pods. A pod is a series of connected cubicles arranged in a circle. Supposedly this type of furniture arrangement helps to grow teamwork, allows the supervisor to hear and see the team's activity, and allows for coworkers to see who is absent or on break. The downside was that we could hear nearly every word spoken by all of us.

One guy had a very loud voice. When he was on a call, all of us could hear every single word he uttered, LOUD and CLEAR. And when he laughed, it was like an annoying honking noise! We all wear headsets that cover one ear and have a microphone in front of our mouth. I actually had several customers ask what was going on because they could hear this guy talking and laughing in the background!

At first, several of us just gave him subtle signals that he was too loud, such as putting an index finger to our lips, or waving our hands downward, hoping he would get the hint to lower his volume. I swear he would get louder after we tried to get him to take it down a notch or two.

I went to our supervisor and asked her to talk to him. In the meeting with the supervisor, he said that he didn't realize or think he was too loud but he would try and talk more softly.

Turns out he had a hearing problem. He couldn't hear himself speaking, so he couldn't judge his own volume. I felt pretty badly after that. Maybe the story should be about me as the worst employee?

Sweet or Savory?

When I was in my early 20s, I worked as a manager for a well-known national cookie store chain inside the food court of our local mall.

One of the marketing tricks to attract people to our store was that the oven fans pushed the smell of the cookies, as they were baking, into the mall walkways. The smell was so powerful that customers literally followed their noses!

We hired an assistant manager, Kristine, to help me as the store was really busy during the holiday season. I was impressed with her as she was a recent college graduate, had an impressive work ethic (showed up early for every shift, very pleasant with everyone), and was able to sell the most cookies per hour of all of us, including me.

It wasn't long before I was very comfortable leaving her in charge of the store for a complete shift. I still had to show up to complete the closing procedures, but I was confident in her abilities to handle the store during normal hours.

One evening as I walked toward the store to start the closing process, I didn't smell the usual delectable waft of dark chocolate, vanilla, and cookie dough. Instead I smelled the aroma of garlic, oregano, and pizza dough. Whoa! Did a pizzeria move into the mall and figured out how to pump the irresistible smell of pizza out to the masses of shoppers just as we had?

As I approached our store, I looked around for this new Italian addition to our mall eateries. But I spied nothing of the sort. Instead, I realized that this delicious smell was incongruously emanating from our ovens—of the cookie store!!

"Kristine, am I smelling pizza instead of cookies coming from our ovens?"

"Yes, on my break I picked up a few slices. I brought them from a pizza joint near my house before coming to work. They got cold as I was selling about another six dozen cookies. So I thought to throw them in the ovens for a few minutes to reheat them. Good pizza too. I just moved here from New Jersey, and I really miss the pizza."

I gently coached Kristine about the power of the smell of cookies, not pizza, drifting through the mall. But because she was a top cookie salesperson, and it was near the end of the shift, I didn't make a big deal about it. A pizza place did open in the mall shortly after that. I wonder if she had anything to do with it!

I'm One of the Worst

I was the worst employee! Yup. It was me. I did many of the annoying, crazy, stupid, and mean things listed in this book.

I was just trying to fit in, have fun, get noticed, push others away, or attract others to me. It took me years to realize that I was the problem.

Truthfully, how I finally came to understand that I was the problem, was when a supervisor took the time to talk to me. She wasn't my supervisor. She worked in a completely different department. She and I didn't have a lot of previous interactions or contact, so it was kinda odd when she called me to her office one morning.

"I wanted to talk to you, one-on-one, because you remind me of myself when I was starting out at the company." She went on to tell me a lot of stories that did, indeed, sound like me.

"I too, tried many roles to justify my behavior—the department comedian, dysfunctional diva, and arrogant top producer. But the real me, the authentic me, deep down, was tired of pushing and pulling people away. It was exhausting. It was only when I committed to being a kind, consistent, contributing member to my team members, did the real success come. If you're willing, I would like to be a champion of your future success. It's similar to having me as a mentor, but more like a supporter of the hard work that you will be responsible for."

That one simple conversation changed my whole life.

I hope this book does the same for others, like me, who struggled with how to succeed in the modern workplace.

Chapter 10

ALLIGATOR

> **Change is inevitable. Whether you think it is positive or negative, you are right.**

It is important in our personal and professional lives that we become committed to our mission but remain flexible regarding our method. Our company, Narrative Television Network, for over thirty years has made TV, movies, and educational programming accessible to the 13 million blind and visually impaired Americans and millions more around the world. As a blind person myself, it has been, and continues to be, a privilege to develop and distribute this life-changing service.

We create an additional soundtrack that is edited into the original programming between the existing dialogue. This additional soundtrack describes the settings, actions, and other visual elements on the screen. In this way, blind people can hear what they can't see. It's like having a sighted friend sitting beside you to tell you what's going on. When we launched our company in the late 1980s, we created soundtracks using reel-to-reel audio recorders. We actually cut tape with razor blades and spliced it back together using Scotch tape. This was the state-of-the-art at the time to deliver our accessible soundtracks. Throughout the years the technology has advanced, so we have gone from reel-to-reel to VHS to beta to 3/4" tape to digital files delivered via satellite.

And today, our accessible soundtracks live somewhere in a computer and are delivered via technology I can't begin to understand much less explain. Our mission is still to open the world of visual media to blind and visually impaired people, but our methods have gone from horse and buggy to Star Trek.

The Curmudgeon

My mother always said, "Don't judge a book by its cover and never judge a person by their outward appearance." But she never met Mr. Z at my job at an insurance company!

I was in my mid-20s when I was hired by a nationally-recognized insurance company in the claims department as an adjuster. Wide-eyed, yet deeply determined to be a high-performer, I set about learning all I could to exceed established goals, impress my boss, and advance my career.

While nearly everyone I worked with was friendly, there was one guy who seemed to be a loner. Everyone referred to him as "Mr. Z," because his last name began with the letter Z and was really tough to pronounce. He was probably in his late 60s and had worked for the company for nearly thirty years. Behind his back, a few of my coworkers called him Mr. G instead of Mr. Z because he came off as such a grouch!

Mr. Z rarely smiled, never spoke first, ate lunch alone, never attended after-work social events, and just gave off a nonverbal vibe that he didn't want to be bothered by anyone.

I thought he was scary.

Only years later, long after I left that job, did I find out that he was slowly losing his hearing, wouldn't (or couldn't) buy hearing aids, and didn't want to talk so that he wouldn't misunderstand conversations.

I guess my mom was right, I shouldn't have judged a book by its cover.

Negative Ned

We have all heard of the Negative Nellie character at work. Well, I worked with the male counterpart, Negative Ned.

Negative Ned had twenty-two years in with our employer, a small manufacturer. As the controller of the company, he never, ever, on any day, at any meeting, during the course of my tenure there (about seven years), ever had a positive, hope-filled response to any new idea, concept, or thought.

His vocabulary was limited to "No," "Never," "Won't work," "Can't afford it," "Let's not be the first to try out a new idea," "We tried it in the past and it failed." Ned truly never had an innovative, forward-thinking, visionary thought in his life. I was convinced he thought it was his role to actually put the brakes on great ideas.

I quit after eight months.

Resisting Change

I supervise a team of eight people, all of whom spend their workdays maintaining the safe and efficient operation of a very large manufacturing plant. These people are highly trained, long-tenured engineers who take great pride in their work.

Because of the sheer size of the operation, I occasionally communicate with them via text messages. If I need to communicate a quick, brief message, it really is quite convenient to just send all eight of them a short text.

I had been using text messaging with them for about three months when I realized a pattern was developing. Omar (not his real name—not even close), would occasionally say, "I didn't get the text," or "Can't you just email me instead of texting?" Omar would miss a meeting or fail to respond to a text message.

One afternoon, I needed to assemble them all together for a quick update. I sent a text message asking that they all report to the conference room in an hour. Omar didn't show.

After hunting him down and getting him to the meeting, I asked, "Omar, did you get my text about this meeting?" He shook his head and looked down at the table.

One of his team mates spoke up and said, "He won't use his cell phone."

Our company issues and pays for a cell phone to all the plant employees in our department, so I knew he had one. "Omar, why won't you use your cell phone?"

He calmly states, "I refuse to learn how to use it. We did perfectly well before these stupid things were invented and we can do well without them now. I'm not going to let myself get addicted to it like everyone else. I'm 64 years old and this ol' dog is not interested in learning any more new tricks."

After the meeting, I spoke privately with Omar about his resistance to using his cell phone. He admitted to being intimidated by it and simply didn't want to adapt to any new technology because he thought he would embarrass himself by his lack of knowledge. "Omar, you are perfectly confident and competent maintaining this billion-dollar manufacturing operation. You are certainly capable of using this silly ol' cell phone!"

I spent fifteen minutes showing him how easy it was. And you know what really hooked him and brought him over to the modern side of phones? When I showed him how to have live video chats with his grandkids!

Omar finished by saying, "Okay, now I'm addicted too! Seeing and speaking to my grandkids, live, is wonderful!"

Generational Gap

For six years I worked as production supervisor for a manufacturing company that produces specialized pipe for the natural gas industry. When I started work with them, they were celebrating their 75th year in business and there were many employees who had worked there for forty years and more.

When I started in my role as a supervisor, I was 31 years old. I had five direct reports, and three of them had each worked for this company for thirty-five years or more. That meant that these three employees each had more years of tenure with this one employer than I was old! All three of these specific employees had children, even grandchildren, my age. And one of them (I'll call him Will), really struggled with our age difference.

As a millennial, I knew that my generation was often the brunt of media-hyped myths such as "Millennials are lazy, won't work overtime, are addicted to their cell phones, etc." Well, I was certainly not any of those things. Plus, I have had excellent mentors and training on effective strategies for working with a generationally diverse workforce. So to some extent, I expected some of the pushback when I was assigned to this role as their supervisor.

Since I strongly believe in a servant leadership approach to supervising, every one of my employees was very respectful and receptive to my direction, especially when they repeatedly saw me get my hands dirty along with them, work overtime, and always give them the credit when things went well, as I took sole responsibility when they didn't. Except Will. He would flippantly call me "Son," "Boy," or "Young Man." He would blatantly go against my recommendations and requests.

I made multiple attempts at one-on-one discussions with Will, as I tried to understand the underlying issues as to why he so openly resented being supervised by someone half his age. I even told him that I could understand these challenges and that many American companies were having similar generational gap issues as four generations were now in the workplace.

I remember even telling him that, "I respect your extensive tenure and want to learn from you. And as a servant leader, my commitment is to you."

Will retired that following year. He never did really acclimate to our age differences. Some of his peers shared that he was raised "old school" and even raised his own family in a similar manner.

Don't Be Afraid, Be Prepared

I work for an internationally renowned Fortune 100 company. We hire only the most accomplished professionals and the brightest minds from Ivy League colleges.

Our engineering department is a cache of geniuses. They are so smart that some of my colleagues, who are not in the engineering department, admit they are intimidated by them. Ironically, some of the engineers admit that are very uncomfortable speaking with people they don't know and are panicked by the thought of ever having to speak in front of a group.

About three months ago, the VP of the research and development team decided that he wanted to showcase some of the projects his engineers were working on. He was proud of their work and wanted more departments to appreciate their skills. So he asked several of the project managers to prepare a thirty-minute presentation to be delivered to the executive team, including the CEO and CFO. It didn't take long for the terror, anxiety, and paralysis to set in, due to their fear of speaking in front of others.

One engineer, who was uncharacteristically more vocal than his peers, threatened a mutiny. He said, in a tone of great indignation, "My project team is *not* going to present anything in front of people who are not engineers because they won't understand it. And secondly, we are not being paid to put together PowerPoint slides, stand in front of a gaggle of big wigs, and be judged for our verbal communication skills as if we were some cheesy motivational speaker like Tony Robbins or Zig Ziglar!"

My first silent reaction was, "Whoa! I love Tony Robbins and Zig Ziglar, and if I could be as compelling and influential as them in front of a group, my career would soar!"

Here's how this ended (and I have to give our executive team a lot of credit for their positive-minded response): The highly vocal engineer was asked to be part of a team of fellow engineers who sought out a professional presentation skills coach. With the assistance of that presentation skills coach, all the engineers participated in a two-day workshop where they were taught very specific insights into the art and science of being a powerful presenter. Every engineering team member was able to deliver an impressive program including the dude who nearly lost his job due to his fear of speaking in front of others.

Chapter 11

CAMEL

It's great to have things as long as our things don't have us.

When we learn something, we can change our own life. When we teach something, we can change another's life—but when we teach people to teach, we can change the world. Having tools, knowledge, or information in the workplace that is not freely shared can become a burden not an asset. As the coauthor of this book, with my esteemed colleague Kristine Sexter, I'm embarrassed to admit to you that when I could read books with my eyes, as you are reading these words on a printed page or electronic screen, I don't know that I ever read a whole book cover-to-cover. After losing my sight, I discovered audio books and helped to pioneer the technology behind high-speed digital audio listening. Today, as a blind person for thirty years, thanks to this amazing technology, I read a complete book virtually every day. This has changed my life in countless ways.

Among my favorite genres of books to read are historical novels. I remember reading an account of one of the pioneers who regularly traveled from the plains of Kansas through the Rocky Mountains and into California, then he would return the following spring. When he first began these journeys, he only had his horse, a pack mule, and a few supplies. Throughout the years, he acquired more possessions and was forced to begin traveling in a wagon to carry all of his stuff. This made it impossible for him to travel through the cool mountain passes each summer. Instead, he was forced to take a much longer route through the desert during the hottest time of the year in order to reach his destination. After several years of these trips, the pioneer realized that all of the things he acquired had become a curse and not a blessing.

If you are part of a team in the workplace, all the information, resources, contacts, and expertise you have should benefit the team.

Holding Her Knowledge Hostage

After getting my Master's degree in Human Relations from a state college, I was so excited to join a small but very well-known, highly respected manufacturer in my small home town in Texas.

About two months after I started, the owner came to me with an unusual request. "I have a big problem and I don't know what to do," he said. I eagerly awaited his description of his challenge as I was excited to show that I was ready to help, maybe be a hero, too!

"She has been here as our only accounting employee for thirty-four years. Over the course of those years, the accounting software system grew to become a convoluted pile of combined software programs written back in the 1980s, along with newer, more mainstream accounting packages. But the real problem is that she has announced that she is retiring in thirty days. And she refuses to train a successor! I'm freaking out. She is the only one who knows how to run the entire accounting program!"

My first thought having heard this? I was shocked! And not with her. There was obviously some kind of passive aggressiveness happening with her, but how irresponsible to be the owner of a $10 million business and not realize that you can't have sole sources of knowledge!

My very first response to him was, "So, who ran the accounting department when she was on vacation or sick?"

"No one. For the past thirty years, she took her vacations during holidays and was rarely, if ever, absent. She really has been a rock of reliability. And now she announces today that she is retiring in a month!? When I asked her to stay long enough for us to hire someone to replace her and enough time to train the new accountant, she simply said, 'Thirty days is my notice. Two weeks is the norm, so I am already giving you more notice than the norm.' She turned around and walked out of my office."

Knowing there are two sides to every conflict, I went to her office. It didn't take long to learn that she was very resentful of her employer. Apparently, she was promised a significant raise, an assistant, and a company truck about ten years prior. None of it ever materialized. She admitted never following up, nor asking about this so-called promise. Instead, she spent the last ten years letting this unfulfilled promise fester into a deeply held cancer of resentment. And her revenge was to hold her knowledge hostage!

It was sad. She left just two weeks later after blowing up at the owner. After thirty-four years, her lasting legacy could have been so positive, but instead she will be remembered for how she exited.

Musical Genre Wars

We work in a small office of eight people. We are in cubicles in a large room, but once we are seated in our chairs, the cubicle walls are tall enough that we can't actually see one another.

One morning, one of my coworkers brought in a small portable radio and starting playing music. It was just loud enough that we could all hear it, but it was not so loud that it was a distraction. For about the first day it was nice. Except all she played was country music! I hate country music! No, I actually loathe country music! Fingernails scraping a blackboard would have been more tolerable over country music!

On day number three, I couldn't help myself. I went to my coworker and politely asked, "Can we change the station for a little more variety?" Her response, "Well, it's my radio and I love this country station."

"OOOOkkkkkkkaaaayyy," was what my brain said. The war is on. The next day, I brought my own radio. And I tuned to my favorite classic rock station and placed the volume just a tiny bit louder than the country music. Really, I promise, it was just a smidge louder than her grating country junk, just so that I couldn't hear hers.

Guess what happened next? Two of my coworkers also brought in their own radios the following week. One played a classical station, and the other sports talk radio. Now, four of the eight of us had our own radios each playing something different.

At this point, together these four radios did create a bunch of distracting noise. The manager said, "No more radios."

I blame that first country-music-loving coworker, who refused to share the airwaves.

Chapter 12

AMOEBA

> **Regardless of how intelligent we may be, if we make stupid choices, we will suffer the consequences.**

I have long believed that we don't fail because we don't know what to do. We fail because we don't do what we know. Many of us here in the 21st century are guilty of having much information, a lot of education, and very little wisdom. Knowledge is the process of acquiring information. Wisdom is the process of applying knowledge. Think of all the times when you have made a mistake or done something stupid and heard yourself say, "I knew better than that."

In the workplace, we don't only think and act for ourselves, we think and act for those we serve, our colleagues, and the entire organization. I have been part of an accountability group for more than twenty-five years with several individuals whom I highly respect both personally and professionally. I have gotten in the habit of running decisions past them before I act, and this practice has paid great dividends on a number of occasions.

It's good to have a mastermind of caring and knowledgeable people around you. While it can be uncomfortable to share your thinking with them before you act, it pales in comparison to the embarrassment of making a poor decision and then having to tell your dream team about it later. In the workplace, we become known for the decisions we make.

Telephone, Telegraph, Tell Curtis

Curtis is known as "Mr. Nosy." He is so nosy that he would often open up conversations with, "So, got any juicy gossip for me today?" He seemingly had to be in "the loop" on all the gossip and rumors at work. When he wasn't able to cajole any juicy tidbits from others, it was well known that he would simply make something up!

The hiring team brought on a new employee, let's call her Tabitha, to work the third shift (11 p.m. - 7 a.m.). Tabitha struggled working the night shift. It can be difficult to switch to a routine that is opposite from the traditional work and sleep schedule for most adults.

One evening, Curtis, who also works the third shift, announces that Tabitha is taking naps in the stalls of the ladies restroom. I asked Curtis, "Exactly how do you know that?" He flatly stated, "I'd watch her go into the ladies room, I'd wait fifteen minutes, and then go in. I can hear her snoring."

Curtis, aka Mr. Nosy, doesn't work with us anymore. And Tabitha, after some coaching, has become a bright-eyed, very effective third shift employee.

It's My Phone's Fault

Me: "Why are you forty-five minutes late to work this morning?"

Employee: "It's not my fault. My alarm didn't go off. "

Me: "Well, aren't you the one who sets the alarm?"

Employee: "No, Siri does."

Dee, You Eye, Okay?

Dee was a wonderful employee. The kind who came to work on time, met all her deadlines, and was friendly to all her coworkers.

She had worked for the company for about eighteen months when one afternoon, as the lunch hour was ending for her and her department's team, there was a wail of police sirens outside our office windows. Since this is a small town, the sound of police sirens, particularly so close to our building, caused all of us to run to the windows.

"Whoa! Is that Dee? The cops have her in handcuffs and are putting her into the back of the police car!"

Her immediate supervisor ran outside to see what was happening. "Officer, what's happening here? This lady is one of my employees."

"Ma'am, this lady is under arrest for driving under the influence. She was caught stealing alcohol from the liquor store, filling up empty Gatorade bottles with it, and then proceeding to drive back to her place of employment here, while crossing the center line. She failed the sobriety test. Badly!"

We later discovered that Dee's Gatorade bottles in the breakroom refrigerator were all filled with her special brew.

Worst Decision

When I was in college, my best friend and I worked together during the summers at a local restaurant. It was an expensive, upscale steak restaurant that attracted affluent couples and business people looking to impress their customers or clients. The tips were so good that we didn't have to work during the school year as long as we socked away our money.

After one very long, yet fiscally successful shift, my best friend says that she is going to meet up with a guy for a drink that she met that night. He had dined at the restaurant that night and had hit on her. He left her a hundred-dollar tip.

I begged her not to go. I reminded her that we had a pact to never date customers.

Fast forward, she went. He took her out about five or six times during the month before college restarted. She gushed about how rich he was, how he bought her small, expensive trinkets, and that he spent tons of money on dinners with her. "I think I'm in love with him! If he asks me to move in with him, I think I will do it. I can finish college later." In disbelief I shouted, "Your parents will totally kill you! You have to finish college! You don't even really know this guy!"

The next night at work, a woman comes storming into the restaurant yelling and screaming that her husband's "girl-friend works here! Where is she?! I'm going to kill her!" She was waving her phone around showing a picture of my best friend in an intimate embrace with her new man. Except he wasn't "her man," he was married!

Our manager was smart enough to steer the woman back outside, as I quickly grabbed my friend and pushed her into the kitchen.

We both returned to college three weeks later. My friend learned a lot that summer, particularly that her education needed to be her priority. So while she was once a "worst employee," she was still my best friend.

High Dollar Driver

Our company's president owns a $20 million private jet. She also owns three exotic supercars worth, collectively, about $500,000. She stores all of these prized possessions in a hangar at the airport. As a reward to certain employees, she invites one or two of us to drive the exotic supercars around the general area or park them in the hangar when the jet is being repositioned.

My coworker and I were invited to do just that. We were so incredibly excited. Not because we won the latest contest, but because we got to get behind the wheel of one of her supercars!

Guess what my worst fellow employee did? Backed the Lamborghini into the jet. Yup. He was so distracted by the whole experience, he hit the jet with the back of the Lambo.

Say bye-bye to this perk. She never again invited any of the employees to the hangar. The guy kept his job, but I heard that the insurance company had to pay over $200,000 in damages to fix the plane and the car.

Chapter 13

LEOPARD

> **We will become known for the good traits we consistently exhibit or the bad habits we allow to creep into our life.**

I find it ironic that half of the true stories in this section deal with individuals who couldn't get to work on time. I have dealt with this in my own company and, as we are a television and movie post-production studio, our final product is the result of a collaboration from a lot of people. Writers interact with narrators who interact with engineers, but when one of the narrators can't get to work on time, the whole train grinds to a halt. I'm not referring to the occasional flat tire or traffic jam kind of tardiness. I'm referring to people who have elevated being late (or other bad habits) to an art form. If you remove all of the excuses for their lack of punctuality, they will still be late.

There's a time in human behavior when a destructive act becomes a habit and then brands us in such a way that we become known for this trait. If you stretch the truth enough, you'll become known as a liar. If you repeatedly take things that don't belong to you, you will be known as a thief. Or if you constantly keep everyone waiting for you to arrive, that behavior will become your identity.

These spots on our performance can overshadow our value as an employee and even our worth as a person. Think of the world leaders, great artists, and award-winning performers who are now permanently known for a single moral lapse or weak judgement.

Shifting Shifts

Our company is staffed around the clock. So we hire for all three shifts: 8 a.m. to 4 p.m.; 4 p.m. to midnight; and midnight to 8 a.m. The most requested shift, not surprisingly, is the traditional first shift, 8 a.m. to 4 p.m.

We hired AJ (not his real name) for the second shift, 4 to midnight, because he requested it. We pay extra for those who work either the second or third shift as an incentive for recruiting and keeping those who want these nontraditional worktimes. So we were really happy to offer AJ the role after his references checked out.

In his first forty days, he was late—at least fifteen minutes—twenty-two out of those forty days.

After speaking with him, he shared that his kids' drop-off times to school and preschool really made it difficult for him, nearly impossible, to get to work by exactly 8 a.m. So we allowed him to start work at 8:15 as long as he worked until 4:15 p.m.

I bet you know what's coming. AJ wasn't quite able to get to work on time even after he was given special privileges to arrive at 8:15 a.m. AJ started arriving at 8:25, then 8:35. His coworkers, who were already miffed that he was granted permission to start late, became more vocal about AJ's persistent tardiness.

During his exit meeting, AJ admitted he has always struggled to get to appointments, work, and even special family events on time. He said that his family members lie to him about the start times of things simply because they know he always runs late.

Highly Opinionated

I work for a wonderful organization that is very committed to the core values of integrity, team work, and diversity. They go so far as to ask the HR department to remove names, addresses, and any other information that might reveal gender, age, socioeconomic, ethnic, or cultural background on all resumes so as to avoid bias in hiring. This has resulted in a company that really is a mosaic of all types of people.

We hired this one person (I won't say if male or female) who, openly and frequently, shared that they were raised in a very strict household and were taught to never accept gay marriage as normal. What this person did not know was that I am gay and married to my partner.

I never did tell this person the truth of my marriage. However, I suspect someone else did as this person made great efforts to avoid me. And I was fine with it.

It's All in the Timing

I work with a person who simply, absolutely, never, ever can get to work on time. I am not talking about the occasional ten-minutes late to work when there is an unusual traffic jam or snowy rush-hour morning. I am talking about an every-single-day-Monday-through-Friday kind of late.

My coworker even jokes about it with us and our supervisor. "You know me, I can never get to work on time. I have always been this way. My family even lies to me about the time things start or when we need to be somewhere, knowing that I am never anywhere on time."

Arghhh! I am the type that if I am fifteen minutes *early* to work or an appointment, I feel I am late. This coworker drives me insane.

Annoying Silence

When most people think of "worst employee" stories, I suspect they envision the obnoxious, loud, egotistical, control freaks (or maybe that's the typical "worst bosses" story?!).

My story is of someone quite the opposite: silent, passive, and unresponsive.

I work in the information technology field creating software for specialized industries. Much of our day is spent in front of our computers, alone in our offices. When we have department meetings, our manager does most of the talking. When we are asked a question or are solicited for our opinion, everyone opens up and contributes, except Jesse.

Jesse won't make eye contact, will just nod or shake his head as a response to a close-ended, yes or no question. If an open-ended question is directed to him, he tends to just shrug his shoulders or murmur something like, "I dunno."

We didn't know anything about him at all. We would try and engage him in the occasional conversation, but it was obvious that he was painfully uncomfortable having any type of casual exchange.

I would sometimes imagine who Jesse really was. What was he hiding? Was he part of the witness protection program? A spy? Hiding from an ex-wife or girlfriend?

We never did find out. He disappeared. Simply didn't show up one day. Poof! Gone...

Chapter 14

RAVEN

> If we're going to succeed in our
> personal and professional lives, we
> have to know the difference between
> the two and act appropriately.

M ost of us spend more time with our colleagues and coworkers than we do with our families. Obviously, it is positive in the workplace when individuals form friendships and create a pleasant working environment, but we need to make sure we understand the difference between a personal and professional relationship. Many professional relationships have been ruined when the individuals involved extended the relationships into their personal lives. Conversely, many friends or relatives who were excited by the idea of working together, found the reality to be much different once they interacted on the job.

As in most human endeavors, the Golden Rule can guide us. "Do unto others as you would have them do unto you," seems to answer most questions. In the workplace, we want to treat colleagues as we would want them to treat us, our spouse, our parents, or our children. We never get a second chance to make this good first impression.

A Letch

My very first job was, just like millions of other teenagers, in a fast food restaurant. I was so excited. I had just gotten my driver's license and felt so grown up driving the two miles to work. I didn't even mind the neon-colored uniform with the matching hat! Plus, I had the opportunity to work with my best friend from school.

One of my coworkers, who was about twenty years older than us, seemed like a really nice guy at first. He spent a lot of extra time explaining the processes and the products to my friend and me. He was always smiling at us and asking us about our school work, what we did for fun, and what our parents thought of us working there.

At first, I didn't think anything of his extra attention. Until the day that he followed me into the walk-in freezer. Normally, we just leave the freezer door open because we are just dashing in and out to get something. It doesn't have a lock on it anyway so as to make sure no one ever gets stuck in there.

After grabbing a 10-pound bag of frozen french fries, I turned around to leave and there was this guy! He had closed the door behind him and was staring at me. The creep then says, "I can warm you up." I threw the French fries at him and ran out.

I quit right then. I just walked out. I found out later that he had tried the same thing on my friend about thirty minutes prior.

When I shared the story with my parents and Grandma, she said in her day that folks like him were called "letches."

Getting Sweaty with a Coworker

I was working as a personal trainer for a well-known, nation-wide gym. It is not unusual for most of the employees at a gym to be fit and attractive. Most of us wear typical uniforms for the industry: spandex shorts, tight tank tops or t-shirts—all emblazoned with the company's logo.

When the gym hired a new trainer to work specifically in the weight training department, all of us warmly welcomed him and offered our assistance as he learned the day-to-day expectations of his new role.

Alan (not his real name) was the proverbial shy and quiet type. He was polite, very unassuming, and never strutted his ego around the gym as so many others tend to do. For that mere fact, I was attracted to him. One morning as we were preparing for the morning rush, I inquired, "So, Alan, how did you get into bodybuilding?"

Peering softly at me he said, "In the fourth grade I was bullied and beat up by a kid who also terrorized others. While I was humiliated, I was even more pissed off about how he had done the same crap to so many others. I was tired of it. So I asked my dad to teach me how to defend myself."

I was swooning. He was sweet, shy, and strong. And had principles!

Okay, I'll cut to the chase. We got sweaty together.

There's a reason why they say that workplace romances are not a good idea. After about two months, I learned that Alan was "getting sweaty" with three other staff members. I didn't discover it for the two months we dated as we have an unwritten policy that discourages staff from dating. It is a "Don't ask, don't tell" type of policy. That was how he was able to keep us all quiet.

Going to the Dogs

Our company is known for being a cool place to work. No real dress code, flexible hours (as long as you get your work done), and on Friday's we can bring our dogs to work with us.

I have two dogs, so I would alternate which dog I brought to work each Friday. My little dog, named Cessna, is a sweet, calm, fluffy white Bichon Frise who plays perfectly with all other dogs. My other dog is a 14-year-old Lhasa Apso, named Brooke, who because of her age really never moves away from my feet and has no interest in the other dogs on her Friday at my work.

I recognize that the title of this book is *100 Worst Employees*, but my problem was not with a human coworker, but a canine coworker!

Brutus was aptly named. A big, stocky bulldog, Brutus' owner was one of the nicest, kindest coworkers I have ever had the pleasure of working with. But Brutus did what he wanted, ignoring his owner.

The rule was we were to keep our own dogs with us, at our feet, similar to a service dog. And any form of "distraction or disruption caused by a dog" would get that dog dismissed or "dis-dogged" as we teased one another.

But Brutus had other ideas. He rarely stayed calm and would bark and tug at his owner's leash anytime another dog walked by. His owner was able to get him to stop barking pretty quickly so we gave him a few "bark passes."

It wasn't until Brutus got loose one morning from underneath his owner's desk and hightailed it to my feet, where my sweet, old Brooke lay sleeping. Brutus took a flying leap and landed right on top of Brooke causing her to squeal in shock (all dog owners know precisely that sound of a dog's squeal of shock or pain. It is high pitched, piercingly loud, and immediately draws sympathy from all mammals who hear it).

Thankfully Brooke wasn't hurt, but Brutus did get the boot or as we say, "dis-dogged."

Reformed and Too Informed

You know how they say that reformed smokers are the least tolerant of current smokers? I have a coworker who took this concept to an Olympic level!

His deal was not that he quit smoking, but that he lost 100 pounds on some diet. Everyone at work was really supportive of him as we all watched him stay on track. Each Friday morning (his weigh-in day), we would ask him how the weigh-in went and cheer his successes.

So after about sixteen months, he lost 100 pounds. Cool. Great. You did it, dude. But then he became everyone's "registered dietician." He would remark in the breakroom over lunch that someone's food was so high in fat and sugar and calories, and that it was not good for their heart or liver or some other organ. He would walk by our office and make wise cracks about how "nutritionally deficient" sugar-free soda was and how it would "increase sugar cravings...." Gosh, this now-skinny guy was annoying.

I started avoiding him and his crusade to save all the rest of us from gluten, sugar, and fat.

New Employee Hazing

I have been at this job, in the main office at a local high school, for just a few months. It seems my coworkers act worse than the high school students! Right from the start, the staff has been truly unfriendly. I make great efforts to be nice and appropriately friendly, but they still snub me.

Today there is an awards luncheon for one of the cafeteria ladies. Did anyone tell me? No! They all just up and left. I looked around and everyone was simply gone. I had to ask one of the teachers where everyone was. So now it looks like I am snubbing the person being honored. Maybe there is some kind of "pay your dues" type of acceptance here. I hate it. It reminds me of how insecure I felt in high school when I was 17 years old.

I am 43 years old. And I am *not* going to deal with this. I am just going back to selling Avon.

Candidate Conflict

During recent election cycles, the open hostility toward others who did not support the same candidate has gotten out of hand. Our office is small (only twelve people) and we try to have a flexible, family-friendly work environment. We look out for one another and the families of each other.

When there is tension in the office, or some type of unresolved conflict, it impacts all of us. So when we saw that we had varying opinions as to who each of us was going to support in the recent election, we agreed to follow our mothers' advice not to discuss politics or religion in mixed company.

One of our coworker's took the word "discuss" to mean its literal definition to not openly "talk" about politics. He went about plastering each square inch of his cubicle in political signs of the candidate of his choice. He would wear shirts and hats, even socks, emblazoned with slogans and pictures of his preferred candidate. He even had a bobble head depicting his candidate on his desk.

Because he never openly "discussed" politics, he was not technically compromising our agreement. We were just happy when the elections were over. He took all of the political regalia down from his cubicle. He still occasionally wears a hat of this candidate, but we don't acknowledge it.

Chapter 15

HOWLER MONKEY

> When you feel tempted to speak out of anger or frustration, think before you talk. If you're still tempted, think again.

H owler monkeys are known as extremely loud and obnoxious creatures that sleep up to fifteen hours per day—not a good resume to build a career upon. When I launched the Narrative Television Network, I spent several years hosting an on-air talk show where I interviewed actors and movie stars who appeared in the films we were broadcasting. As a result of that experience, I was asked to cohost a political show in Washington, DC with the legendary *Today Show* anchor Jim Hartz. As Mr. Hartz had decades of experience and I was new to the scene, I asked him for any advice. Without hesitating, he responded, "Assume all cameras are on and all microphones are hot."

We've all heard about politicians, athletes, or other celebrities who said the wrong thing at the wrong time to the wrong people. Here in the 21st century, the amount of time we spend on security and surveillance cameras is multiplying, and everyone via their cell phone is ready, willing, and able to capture your weakest moment for posterity.

You've heard it said that, "The pen is mightier than the sword," referring to the power of the written word. While I believe this to be true, the power of the written word is dwarfed by the power of the spoken word. What you say, how you say it, and the specific words you use when you communicate, express more about who you are than what you are saying.

I recently wrote a historical novel entitled *Will to Win* featuring humorist and entertainer Will Rogers. It is currently in pre-production as a movie. Among Rogers' memorable quotes is one of my favorites, "Never miss a good chance to shut up." I have never gotten in trouble for what I didn't say. This is especially true in the workplace.

Hot Mic

For fourteen years, I worked for a federal agency that serves people in need, particularly in times of widespread, weather-related disasters. Quarterly, we were required to participate in a regional staff meeting via conference call. There were ten offices that were part of this region, so about twenty people were together on these calls.

The regional manager who facilitated these calls was very organized and structured. At the beginning of every conference call, he would ask that everyone mute their phones so there would be no background noises distracting whoever was speaking.

Almost without fail, there was usually at least one branch office that didn't mute their phone, and we could all hear background noises, chairs being pulled out, coughing, etc.

During this specific meeting, the regional manager was announcing several promotions among this group. He said, "And now, it is my pleasure to announce that Lee has been promoted to senior branch manager of our Austin office!"

Suddenly, and with tremendous clarity and volume, every one of us heard, "Is he freaking kidding me?! This is a crock of crap! I was supposed to get that promotion, not Lame Brain Lee!"

Silence. Complete silence. The regional manager calmly says, "Richard, apparently you did not mute your phone. Look to receive a call from me in fifteen minutes."

Richard actually kept his job. He made all of the appropriate apologies. Ironically, he wound up reporting to Lee. Richard retired about three years after that incident.

No one ever forgot to mute their phone's microphone again.

Salary Transparency

I went to work for a family-owned trucking company as a logistics specialist. During the interview process, I was specifically looking to see if there were any politics or dysfunction that you so often hear about in family-run businesses. I certainly did not want to get into the middle of something like that.

From what I could learn and see, there was not any sign or clue that this family brought their personal or family drama to the office. I accepted the job.

All was well until about a week before Christmas. I could clearly hear one of the owner's sons shouting, nearly screaming, at his brother. They were in the middle of a staff meeting that included all of the family members and five or six others who, like me, were not family members.

Suddenly the conference room door is thrown open, one of the sons stomps across the office to the human resources manager's office, sits down at her computer, and proceeds to email a highly confidential document to every single employee of the company. It was everyone's salary and years of tenure with the company. And it was sorted from the highest paid to the lowest paid.

He fumes as he returns to the meeting, points at his brother, and says to his father, "Now everyone will know that he's always been your favorite!"

Lots of people quit after that.

I stayed on because, frankly, I thought my pay was pretty good. However, it was like walking on egg shells around that place from then on.

Siesta Bookkeeper

I was hired to be the executive director for a wonderful organization. I knew that my approach for the first four to six weeks was to simply get to know all of the staff. I also planned to change nothing until I had a complete understanding of the complete operations.

I was in my second week when I had the opportunity to spend time with the bookkeeper.

I suspect my mouth went agape when I heard this lovely lady, who had been the company's bookkeeper for thirty-eight years say, "At 3 p.m. every day, I will shut my door and take a one-and-a-half-hour nap."

It was such an unexpected statement that my first thought was, "Is she ill?"

"May I kindly ask why you take a one-and-a-half-hour nap each day at work?" I asked.

"Well, it's not *every* day. I will actually take an additional thirty minutes, or a two-hour nap, for the week after daylight savings time."

She retired about two months later.

Cell Phone Groan

Pretty much everyone keeps their cell phone on them at work. This is especially true when your fellow employees are mostly teenagers.

I figured out pretty fast that once I took a job for the summer at a water park, I needed to either leave my phone in the employee locker room or get a waterproof case. Now I admit, I was 19 years old so leaving my cell phone in the locker room was not my first option. So I sprang for a $90 waterproof case.

But not everyone took such precautions. This one girl, who was already known for her diva demeanor, dropped her cell phone right into the rushing water at the top of the log flume tube as she was helping a little kid get situated in his seat.

Her phone traveled along the gushing waters going airborne as it exited at the bottom with a final splash into the pool. I tried to hide my laughter because I know this is a fate that I made efforts to avoid with my new waterproof case, but this girl was such a petty, constant complainer that I did think it was funny.

She freaked out! She went running to retrieve her phone only to confirm exactly what we all knew. Her case-less, already-cracked phone was DOA. She started yelling and screaming to our supervisor, "You have to pay for this! This happened while I was working for you and this stupid place!" The supervisor calmly tried to explain that the phone was her personal property, thus her responsibility. The supervisor reminded her that she even signed a waiver on her first day explaining just that: keep your own personal belongings either in the locker or leave them at home. She quit right then and there. I think the supervisor would have probably fired her anyway because of her uncontrolled, profanity-laden outburst. I think all of us were relieved she was gone.

One last part to this story. The girl's mother started calling the water park every day demanding that her daughter's phone be replaced by them. She even wrote a wicked email to the CEO. The mother made the mistake of putting that same email on her own Facebook page, but even her friends told her she was out of line and wrong. That ended all of that!

Code White

Most people know that a Code Blue means that a patient is in cardiac arrest. But unless you are in the healthcare industry, you probably don't know the other Code colors. For example, a Code Red is for fire. Code Green means that an evacuation is necessary. A Code Black is for a bomb threat.

And a Code White is for a situation in which any individual is behaving in a potentially dangerous manner toward themselves or others and has the potential for escalating, or is escalating, beyond the ability of the present staff to manage the situation.

The craziest Code White I ever saw called was when the wife of one of our emergency room (ER) doctors came storming into the ER, stomping right past all of the admission team members and passing the other ER physicians on a frenzied hunt for her husband.

"Where is he?! Where is the slime ball?!" Shouting at the top of her lungs, she ran from curtained-off area to the next, dragging three 55-gallon trash bags full of clothes behind her.

"I know he's here somewhere! I bet he's hiding in some supply closet! And not alone!"

She proceeded to rip open each of the three trash bags, shaking their contents onto the floor of the emergency room area. Her husband's clothing was strewn all over the floor in a huge heap.

As she was shouting profanities and expletives about her husband's dalliances, security was able to corral her toward a closed off area out of earshot of waiting patients. It was quite the show, embarrassingly so.

Moments later, "Dr. Feelgood" (a name the wife was shouting as she emptied all of his belongings onto the floor) emerged; indeed, from a supply closet where he was hiding from his wife when he saw her coming. He was carrying three new large trash bags (garnered from said supply closet), which he used to repack all of his clothing decorating the floor of the ER.

The Toilet Talker

This one lady I work with always talks to whoever is in the bathroom at the same time. She knows that the ladies room is reserved for our company only, so anyone who is in there is one of her coworkers. She goes into the stall, closes her door, and then says something like, "Is that you Kacy? I can tell it is you because of your fabulous shoes. So how's it going today?"

I think to myself, *How's it going? That's quite an odd question to ask someone who is in the bathroom.* If you don't answer her, she moves on to another subject like the weather or worse, a coworker. She gossips about our coworkers while taking care of business in the ladies room!

One time she said something pretty catty about another coworker, and that person was actually in the bathroom at the same time and heard her!

Please girls, no need to conversate while we urinate!

Chapter 16

MOSQUITOES

Annoying behavior is magnified and multiplied in crowded elevators and airplanes as well as in the workplace.

All of us enjoy private time in our own personal space. This is when we can think anything or say anything. This environment does not exist in the workplace. Not only are we sharing space with our colleagues, we have combined our hopes, dreams, and ambitions with theirs. The old adage that your freedom to swing your arm ends at my nose seems to apply here.

Your colleagues have five senses, and if you abuse the shared workplace environment, you can assault all of those senses. You are entitled to your own faith, political views, food preferences, artistic style, and manner of expression; however, we must never exercise these in the workplace in such a way that it infringes on the rights or freedom of any of our colleagues. People may be offended by thoughts, words, or actions that do not offend you. You must remember that you're not in your own home, you're in everyone's workplace.

When you're not sure how something will be perceived or accepted, remember—*when in doubt, leave it out.*

Not Adept at Adapting

Felecia was frantic and frenetic. All the time. She spent every hour of every workday in a seemingly rushed and highly stressed state. She struggled to get to work on time, missed deadlines, and misplaced items nearly every day.

Felecia struggled to care for herself including the basic need to eat. She often forgot to bring her lunch; or when she did bring a lunch, she'd forget to eat—then she was grumpy and noticeably more disorganized in the afternoon.

She would interrupt others multiple times a day, would forget to take care of tasks assigned to her, and didn't always stay current on her emails and responses. Her obvious anxiety made others around her anxious.

As her manager, I made great efforts to understand her behavior. I understand that human behavior in the workplace is diverse. I am trained to communicate with others in a manner that is calm and result-oriented. I did my best to give her advice and suggestions in a respectful way, which did help her sometimes. However, when I look back over my time with Felecia, I just remember being mentally exhausted most of the time.

Stealing Credit

After relocating from out of state, my new job was to assist with cataloging and general library duties in a school library media center. My library colleague and I were tasked by the administration with making the library more user friendly and inviting to our middle and high school students. After sharing a few ideas that I had implemented in my previous school library position, my colleague was eager to implement some of these same ideas. He and I busily added a soft seating area, made changes in the computer area, and added new signage to the almost nonexistent signage in the shelving areas. The creative and positive changes were evident to all users including staff and administration.

Weekly staff meetings were held in the library, and during one staff meeting the administrator praised my coworker for all the new and exciting changes that had been made. He sat there, glowing from head to toe in the limelight, never mentioning or acknowledging me at all, that these had all been *my* ideas, and that we had implemented them together. He took all the credit. I said nothing.

I left that school a year later. My coworker, although nice to my face, apparently did not realize that if he would have given credit to others, to the team, it not only builds that all-important teamwork, it actually makes *him* look bigger.

Not My Mom

At practically every job I ever worked, there was always a sign on the office refrigerator, "Clean up after yourself. Your mother does not work here!"

At my last job, there was a lady who had worked for the company for more than thirty years and everyone called her "Mom." She seemed to enjoy having her coworkers, especially those who were much younger than her, call her mom. I was not among them.

While I was about thirty years younger than the woman, I just didn't feel comfortable calling her mom because I reserved that title exclusively for my real mom. My real mom is my hero, and I really didn't want to so easily share that name with anyone else.

One day, office mom, whose real name is Louise, asked me, "Why don't you just call me 'Mom' like everyone else? 'Louise' makes me feel so old, plus I like being everyone's work mom."

I simply said, "My mom is my hero and I want her to be the only one with that name."

Louise just stared back at me. Her eyes filled with tears. She didn't respond for almost a minute. "That is the sweetest thing I ever heard." I smiled back at her and went back to my work area.

Several of my coworkers who saw our exchange told me later that Louise made them feel uncomfortable too, and that her attempt to have all younger employees call her mom kind of creeped them out.

If I See It, I Can Share It

As an HR professional for more than fifteen years, I have seen the evolution of many organizational policies go from being mainstays to objects of confrontation.

For example, the Protection of Intellectual Property Agreement, a common, widely used form that stipulates that in the event an employee should separate from the organization (for any reason), they agree to not disclose, divulge, nor discuss proprietary information once away from the organization.

No biggie? Right? Well, this guy was in day two of his employment with our Fortune 500 organization. We were presenting and explaining the usual forms to several new hires during onboarding. As we finished the explanation of the Protection of Intellectual Property Agreement, this new hire abruptly exclaimed, "If I see it, I can't 'un-see it,' so how can you stop me from talking about it? Hahaha!"

His comment that day was quite prophetic. He went on to have the same flippant response to quite a few other things. He was politely separated not too long after his original hire date.

At least he didn't get the chance to see too much that he had to "un-see!"

One-Upmanship

I work with a dude who can't stay out of any conversation and always has to "one up" any situation. At first it was funny, and we just laughed at him behind his back. I saw him as being an insecure young man. But then it became predictable—if someone had a story, he had one that was better or worse.

One day he asked why I was so grumpy. I told him that my childhood dog, Buster, had died and that this dog was my "brother and best friend when I was going through high school."

His said, "Ah heck, that's nothing! Walk it off bro, it's just a dog. I lost a cow once, but heck, we were ranchers! Right?! Get it? A cow. We raise beef!"

Never spoke to this guy again. He quit about six months later to work at his family's cattle ranch.

Chapter 17

TURKEY

> In the workplace when it's all said and done, there is often too much said and not enough done.

M y academic training is in the behavioral sciences with a combination of psychology and sociology. I remember reviewing a patient profile in abnormal psychology. I asked the professor why this individual reacted in a certain way. His response stayed with me and speaks to our study of employees. He said, "Jim, when you're dealing with the way people think and act, you must remember—some people simply get it, and other people don't." Whatever we deem the term "get it" to mean, this wisdom certainly applies in the workplace.

I have a colleague in the National Speakers Association with whom I have collaborated on several projects. One day, we had a scheduled call regarding an audio training program we were doing together. He seemed a bit emotional and somewhat distracted. When I inquired about it, he explained that he had just sent his youngest son off to college the previous day. He described to me that he and his son had spent a great morning together, then they packed the car, and he went out to hug his son and tell him goodbye.

I asked my colleague if he had any parting words of wisdom for his son. When he confirmed that he did, I paid close attention as this particular colleague and friend is a highly respected author and speaker. He told me that he tried to give his son some universal wisdom that would apply to all situations throughout his life. When I asked if he would share it with me, he replied, "I told my boy, 'Wherever you go, whatever you do, and whatever happens, don't be an idiot.'"

At first I found this advice somewhat flippant and quite humorous, but after further consideration I realized that the wisdom "Don't be an idiot" applies to us all, especially in the workplace.

Couldn't Curb His Appetite

When I relocated my family to a small town so I could be the business manager for a utility company, one of the first people to come by the office to meet me was the friend of the previous business manager—who had been there thirty-five years! She wanted to introduce herself, invite our family to church, and let me know her husband was the head of the highway patrol for the region, just in case I needed anything. Oh, and by the way, she wanted me to know that her son was one of the meter readers who worked for me! Interesting. I guessed in a small town like that, everyone knew everyone and looked out for one another.

"Sonny," as I'll refer to him, was a nice enough fellow. He came to work on time, left the office to do his work on time, and returned at the end of the day having completed his meter reading route. He was one of three meter readers for the area.

Although our office was in a very small town, we were responsible for a wide geographic area. All three meter readers stayed busy every day traveling to remote areas to visually "read" the meters and record the information on an electronic device. The devices were then "docked" at the end of the day so the readings could be uploaded to the main computer system. These people had to be willing to work alone, drive in some fairly rugged terrain, and read meters accurately.

The electronic devices the meter readers used tracked the time of the reading and also compared the reading to the previous month's reading as a quality control and accuracy check. I, as the manager, received a daily recap from the day before. Pretty boring reading, if you ask me. However, the reports would allow me to review the accuracy and efficiency of the employees' efforts. Keeping up with the meter readers was actually a fairly small part of my job, so a cursory look at the reports was all that was needed for these three employees. They were honest and dependable, right?

Time marched on and nothing changed for a few months. Everyone in the office was doing their jobs well: customer representatives, cashiers, field personnel. I went about doing my work as a community leader—becoming involved in the Chamber of Commerce, Rotary Club, Sertoma, city hall meetings—all the things that a small town business manager was expected to do. I would occasionally run into Sonny's mom or dad around town.

Then suddenly, Sonny's mom started stopping by the office two or three times a week to check on Sonny—sometimes with his dad in uniform. Sonny was married, had two kids, and lived right down the street from the office. It was odd. Then I started noticing some equally odd information on the daily meter reading reports. Being new to this kind of work, I had been trained recently in things to be aware of with people who handled customer payments and those who dealt with the public. The meter reading reports told me a lot. For most days of the past two weeks, forty meter readings had been entered in the device each day within five minutes. Wasn't this what I had been told was evidence of "curbing"— when a meter reader sat on a curb and made up readings!

Putting some things together—Sonny's late arrivals back at the office most days in recent weeks, the pattern in the daily reports, and his mom's concerned visits—it didn't take a genius to figure out something was going on. After confronting Sonny with the data and hearing some pretty bizarre excuses, he denied anything was amiss. A little more investigation ensued. It turned out, Sonny was meeting a woman at the local no-tell-motel every afternoon about 2 p.m. I guess he figured out how to "curb" the meter readings, but not his appetite. Sadly, it turned out that Sonny had gotten mixed up with some unsavory, and illegal, business.

For me, this was a lesson in not ignoring what's right in front of me regarding changes in employee behavior.

Check Your Text Messages

There are many times that text messaging our staff is appropriate and efficient. If our management team needs to send a quick message, they will often do that in a short text to the staff.

As we all know, when we text, the other person now has our phone number and then adds us to their contacts. There have been some instances of "mistaken identity" when a staff member accidentally sends us a text that was meant for their friends or family. They have typically been harmless such as, "Can you pick up the kids," or "I'm running late, but will be there soon." We typically will respond with a funny note letting them know that they have sent the message to the wrong person.

Unfortunately for Shawna, her wrongfully sent text was not so harmless. Shawna was texting to what she thought was a friend, but it was actually her supervisor. She must have chosen the wrong contact. Not only was Shawna having a great time sending texts about the large amount of marijuana and pills she had, but she also attached pictures! Her supervisor responded to the texts letting her know who she was texting, and then called that same phone number to talk to Shawna. When the phone was answered, Shawna had another person say that we had the wrong number but we could hear her in the background. Needless to say, Shawna is no longer working with us, and we reported it to the police!

Sorry, Can't Make It to Work Today

A staff member, Robbi, worked weekends at the home of one of our patients. Robbi is a residential care specialist, working to support the daily lives of adults needing moderate personal and health care. While Robbi was a warm caregiver, she had a problem with calling in with less than a 24-hour notice to report herself as unavailable for her shift.

After some coaching, Robbi showed great improvement in her level of reliability. Unfortunately, it wasn't too long before Robbi wasn't able to make it to her shift. However, in lieu of calling in herself, she asked her friend to call us and let us know that she was not going to make it to work that day. Apparently Robbi had been arrested for a shocking crime about which her friend went into great detail as to what happened! Needless to say, Robbi wasn't able to come back to work.

Decades of Drug Storage

About fifteen years ago, the Food and Drug Administration released its recommendations for proper disposal of unused medications. It recommended that we no longer simply throw away unused medications in our trash or flush them down the toilet. The FDA is recommending that we bring unused medications to retail pharmacies, hospitals or clinic pharmacies, and law enforcement locations. There is also a National Drug Take Back Day that aims to provide a safe, convenient, and responsible means of disposing prescription drugs while also educating the general public about the potential for abuse of medications.

Well, imagine my reaction when conducting an audit and inventory of medications at one of our newly acquired senior living locations to find an *entire* 9-foot-high, 5-foot-wide closet packed from floor to ceiling with old medications and prescriptions! Two days and twenty-seven boxes later, 521 medication bottles were properly disposed of. The oldest bottle in there? Twenty-one years old!

When I asked the supervisor why this was allowed to happen, she responded, "The rules state that we are to *keep* all medications locked and in a safe place."

Apparently she literally interpreted the word "keep" to mean "forever"!

We did quite a bit of training with the staff at this location after that.

Sleeping Soundly at 36,000 Feet

I am a baggage handler for an airline. After nineteen years on the job, I pretty much have seen things that no one believes possible. People think that these type of stories about coworkers are made up. But I am serious when I tell you that this stuff really happens.

As a baggage handler, we have a job that is very physically demanding. It is constant weight lifting, and in all types of weather. If you're out of shape, don't eat well (or enough), fail to stay hydrated, or not getting enough sleep, the job will beat you.

A new guy, okay, a "newer" guy, who had been on the job about six months, disappeared one super cold night after we loaded a Boeing 737-800. The supervisor wanted to relieve him for his break, but no one could find him. We actually have a procedure for exactly this type of event. Similar to an Amber Alert, we have assigned areas of the airport and operations that we are to search. Nothing. He was nowhere.

Guess where he was? In the forward cargo hold of that Boeing 737-800 that just left. Asleep. Actually, he admitted he was drunk. Goodbye to his job. And goodbye to him. And good riddance. This job is too dangerous to not have reliable, alert, and focused coworkers.

Dog Gone Wrong

In college I worked as a dog groomer. My coworker had worked on two white Bichon Frise dogs that day. These two dogs looked very similar. Get this. He sent the wrong dog home with the wrong owner. And the owners didn't realize for about three hours!

Chapter 18

STINK BUG

> We never get a second chance to
> make a good first impression. This
> includes sights, sounds, and smells.

F ew things evoke instantaneous good memories like smells do. It may be our grandmother's fresh bread baking, newly mown grass in the spring, or a blooming flower garden. On the other hand, nothing prompts distasteful memories quicker than bad smells.

Among the great privileges in my life was to have counted legendary Coach John Wooden among my friends and mentors. John Wooden is recognized among the greatest coaches ever, and his teams set records that will never be equaled. His UCLA Bruins won ten college basketball championships in twelve years. This is unimaginable and awe-inspiring to any fan of the game.

Beyond being a great coach, John Wooden was a great teacher and a great man. The first day of practice each year, he'd describe to his players how to put on their socks, and then he demonstrated the technique for them so they would avoid getting blisters. While Coach's lecture and demonstration got a few snickers and eye rolls from his college players, they came to appreciate and love their coach and everything he taught them.

Coach Wooden went on to explain to his team that they would all be training together, traveling together, and living together, so they needed to respect everyone's space and the environment they would be sharing.

At that time and to this day, visiting sports teams often leave the locker room they are assigned a stinking mess. Coach Wooden's lasting admonition was, "We will keep ourselves presentable at all times and leave our environment better than when we found it." This wisdom holds true whether you are a college basketball player or an employee going to work.

Pee Yew

It is lore in the archives of the human resource industry—the dreaded moment when you have to tell a fellow colleague that he or she stinks. Literally! The proverbial body odor, rank, stank, and reek discussion.

I never thought it would be an issue I would ever have to face. I mean, come on, we are in a white collar, suit-and-tie wearing industry. But I recently joined the ranks of HR professionals who had the "you stank" conversation.

Each year in the fall, our office has a Wellness Fair. All of our employees are given free flu shots, blood pressure checks, BMI testing, etc.

One of our managers, who I will simply call "Lou," decided that after he saw his results from the free health screenings that he was going to start a new exercise program. Every morning before work, he would hit the gym to workout. As admirable as his efforts were, his ability to get to the gym with enough time to take a quick shower before coming into work, left a bit to be desired.

Apparently Lou had no idea that as he walked through the office after his morning workouts, sans showers, that he wafted the odors of an entire high school football team after practice in the summer sun. One of his buddy's teasingly said, "Dude, I can tell you worked out today!"

Lou responds, "Really?! Am I looking that good already?"

"No, it's not yet how you look but how you smell."

Lou defensively responds, "I'll take a shower when I get home tonight. No need to get up even that much earlier to take a shower before work. I'd rather sleep in the extra ten minutes."

After about two weeks of Lou's odoriferous presence at work, several of his office mates came to me. "You're HR. You tell him! We've tried. He shrugs us off."

After Googling best practices for the situation, referencing my old HR textbooks, and even calling a fellow HR colleague, I was ready. I went for the "straight to the point" approach.

"Lou, it has come to my attention, literally and personally, that you are working out each morning before work. I want to tell you what an inspiration you are to me! While being an inspiration is wonderful, your post-workout perspiration, is not. May I gently and kindly ask you to discreetly return home right now and bathe? Also, may I recommend that you work out after work or make time to shower before coming into the office should you decide that morning exercises are best?"

About three months later, Lou had dropped more than twenty-five pounds. He started working out after work. And four of us, including me, joined him at the gym. He was, indeed, the inspiration for our perspiration now!

Smells Bad

This is really petty, but the worst coworker I ever had? This man who wore the same aftershave cologne as my ex-husband!

Every time he walked by and I could smell his cologne, I could feel my blood pressure rise and my brain go into defensive mode!

I know how unfair this is, and I tried to like this guy because he had done absolutely nothing for me to dislike him, but I seriously couldn't help myself. Those olfactory senses were so powerful!

Foul!

The accounts payable clerk I supervised was really quite good at his job but smelled like cigarette smoke so badly it reminded me of the old-time corner bars or the smoking lounges that were once in all airports after cigarettes were banned from airplanes.

His eau-de-cigarette stench was so strong I would gag simply standing next to him having a pleasant conversation. He would walk by coworkers, and the wafting odors would linger for some time. People started to complain to human resources. Apparently the HR department said that since he didn't smoke on company property, they had to handle it in a manner similar to how they tell someone that they have bad body odor. (He chewed nicotine gum all day except when he went out for lunch when he would drive down the street to an empty parking lot and chain smoke in his car.)

The company offered him, and everyone else who used tobacco products, smoking cessation support. When that didn't work, he agreed to move his desk to an empty, tiny office. Some of my coworkers were kind of miffed because he got his own office. One guy plotted to not shower for weeks until he got his own office, but that is another story!

Predictably, this man died from lung cancer. Everything in that tiny office had to be thrown away including the company computer, the land line phone, and all of the furniture. The walls had to be repainted with a special paint designed to kill smoke odors.

Dirty Hands

You really want the worst employee? How about the grossest, most disgusting?

She won't wash her hands! Yup. Over the seventeen years I have worked with this (mostly) lovely lady, I have never seen her wash her hands!

Of course, we occasionally bump into each other in the ladies room. In the seventeen years I have known her, I have never personally seen her wash her hands. Others have never seen her wash her hands after using the restroom either. One particularly extroverted coworker, who also noticed this unusual habit, had the hutzpah to chide her, in a lighthearted way, one morning while they were both exiting the restroom.

"Bea, aren't you going to wash your hands? It's flu season as those signs on the mirror are reminding us." Bea had her hand on the door handle, ready to exit the restroom. (Ugggh, can you imagine the germs on that door handle?!)

Bea said, "Nah. I'm good."

Someone hypothesized that maybe she is allergic to the supplied soap or has a phobia or aversion to the stainless steel faucets. But in the past three years, we have installed touchless faucets, touchless hand towel dispensers, and the soap is a pure, hypoallergenic product.

She has yet to offer any insights. It is sad because the reputation of being the "gross hands lady" has impacted how people think of her. No one shakes her hand for any reason.

OO WORST

Chapter 19

LEECH

> **If we focus our efforts and energy on doing our work instead of getting out of our work, everyone wins.**

often think that the hardest work anyone ever does is the effort they put into avoiding work. Even if you can somehow hide or evade doing your job, you still have to endure the boredom for forty hours each week. I can't think of anything that would be more stressful and less fulfilling.

On the other hand, if we focus all of our efforts and energy on the task at hand, the workday flies by, and we feel exhilarated and energized. We can put our head on the pillow that night knowing our talents were fully utilized, and we provided an honest day's work for an honest day's pay. Beyond raises, bonuses, and career advancement, a job well done is its own reward.

Pole Position

We work in a medical office. When staff go on vacation, we contact HR and ask for a "float." Our float pool is comprised of highly talented, well-educated workers whose permanent job is to fill in for absent employees. Because float staff are multitalented and can perform in many different roles, they are paid very well. So when we go on vacation, we can relax knowing that our position is being filled by great professionals.

So when Isis arrived to fill in at the front admission desk, we knew we would be in great hands. On the third day of her filling in, Isis noticed that a fluorescent light was not working above her desk. She didn't want to wait for maintenance to take care of it, so she took it upon herself to find the supply closet that stored new fluorescent bulbs (the long, skinny kind), and replace it herself.

When most of the office was at lunch, she stood up on a chair (with wheels!) to replace the bulb. No one saw her attempt this obviously dangerous maneuver. Only when they heard the horrid sounds of crashing glass and moans of pain did others come running.

Being a medical facility, Isis immediately received top-notch medical care. She had no broken bones, no scratches. She complained of horrific back pain.

Isis complained of the back pain for nearly six months. She no longer worked, anywhere, as her injuries precluded her from doing so.

While none of us knew her well because she had just started with our clinic, we would occasionally call and email her to ask how she was doing. She said that she was nearly bed-ridden and always in pain. And hadn't worked in six months.

Shortly after that conversation with her, we heard that Isis was photographed by a private investigator hired by her jealous boyfriend. She was working in a very physical job that required quite a bit of contortionist talents—as an exotic, pole-dancer in an adult club.

Apparently Isis set up the whole accident scene and had a record of making similar claims with other employers.

Benefits Who?

Having spent my entire adult life as a human resources professional, I must admit that I have seen it all. I probably have more than one hundred stories about "Worst Employees" that could have filled this book all by myself!

Yet in the scheme of them all, the one story I, and many of my friends who are also HR managers, will admit drives us stir crazy, is that of the employee who blatantly, openly, makes a farce of the benefits and time-off policies.

In general, this is the playbook: Let's assume the employee is hired on January 1. By March 31, the new employee has used all of his or her available paid time off. Granted, most employees earn increased paid time off with tenure, but this employee has only been with the organization less than ninety days—but every day, hour, and minute that is available to them as a means to miss work, has been exhausted.

By April, this same employee calls in sick only on Fridays and Mondays for weeks in a row. This occurs even when the employee is not paid for these days off.

We are not heartless. Of all people, HR professionals are very understanding of the many events that may befall us. But when there is a highly (highly!) predictable pattern of "events," it can jade some of us.

By June, we are having to facilitate documented conversations of tardiness, missed project deadlines, continued, unexplained absences, and open hostility, even threats of lawsuits against us as his or her employer.

By July 1, we are forced to terminate an employee we, just a few months prior, hired with great positive expectations.

Chapter 20

THE ZOOKEEPER

> **A successful conductor must work with all the musicians, and a successful employee must work well with all of their colleagues.**

Within these pages, we have given you 100 examples of what not to do. In this way, you will avoid being one of the *worst* employees. The following is a checklist of action steps that will get you well on your way to being one of the *best* employees.

WorkWise Wisdom

- *Be reliable.* Even those with the finest skills, technical abilities, or Ivy League educations can become liabilities in the workplace if they cannot be trusted to come to work each day, on time.

- *Be consistently respectful and pleasant.* Even if you have to fake it. No one wants to work with a jerk, a drama queen or king, or with someone who has an attitude problem.

- *Be a problem solver not just a problem identifier.* Bring two viable solutions to any challenge or problem you wish corrected.

- *Have integrity.* As C.S. Lewis, a 20th century prolific British writer and theologian said, "Having integrity is doing the right thing even when no one is looking." In today's 21st century workplace, with everyone carrying around cell phones with recording capabilities, and security systems hanging from every corner, you probably are, indeed, being watched.

- *If you make a mistake, take responsibility for it and fix it.* Individual employees, leaders, and even entire corporations are expected to be transparent about their mistakes, egregious errors or transgressions. Those who own their mistakes, make great efforts to fix those mistakes, not only recover, but may actually go on to elevate the level of trust others have in them.

- *Be results-driven.* Strive to establish, and accomplish, goals set by yourself and your employer. Be able to get great results both as an individual and as part of a team.

- *Possess the communication skills necessary to resolve basic workplace conflict.* With as many hours as full-time employees will spend with their coworkers, the inevitable, occasional miscommunication, misunderstanding, or conflict will arise. Employees who are able to have a gracious, solution-oriented conversation with coworkers when negative issues arise will garner great appreciation from everyone. Those who gossip, speak disparagingly of others behind their backs, or create a we-versus-them mentality in their workplaces will never be deemed great employees.

- *Be a trust builder.* Modern employers have come to realize that "trust is the new green." A workplace culture fraught with distrust, hypocrisy, or morale issues will never be able to recruit and retain right-fit employees. These companies will continually struggle to remain profitable. Thus, many hiring managers and human resource professionals are strategically seeking employees with a proven track record of reliability, who consistently conduct themselves with respect and kindness, bring realistic solutions to challenges, exhibit integrity and professionalism, can work effectively alone and while on teams, and have the ability to gracefully manage the occasional workplace personality conflict.

Those who exhibit these personal characteristics will earn the priceless reputation as great employees and will always be in great demand!

As you read through this list, you may say, "Really? That's it? Aren't these things 'no brainers'? Just these eight basic qualities are what makes a great employee?"

Yes! Whether it was the failure of a single, teenage employee who simply couldn't get to work on time to a highly skilled, long-term employee who decides one day to lie about a family member's illness as a means to get sympathy (and dollars!) to entire organizations that come tumbling down in a heap of corporate ash because of a lack of respect and integrity at the top, these eight simple characteristics are what separates the *best* from the *worst!*

ABOUT JIM STOVALL

In spite of blindness, Jim Stovall has been a national Olympic weightlifting champion, a successful investment broker, the president of the Emmy Award-winning Narrative Television Network, and a highly sought-after author and platform speaker. He is the author of more than forty books including the bestseller *The Ultimate Gift*, which is now a major motion picture from Twentieth Century Fox starring James Garner and Abigail Breslin. Five of his other novels have also been made into movies with two more in production.

Steve Forbes, president and CEO of *Forbes* magazine says, "Jim Stovall is one of the most extraordinary men of our era."

For his work in making television accessible to our nation's 13 million blind and visually-impaired people, the President's Committee on Equal Opportunity selected Jim Stovall as the Entrepreneur of the Year. Jim Stovall has been featured in *The Wall Street Journal, Forbes* magazine, *USA Today,* and has been seen on *Good Morning America, CNN,* and *CBS Evening News.* He was also chosen as the International Humanitarian of the Year, joining Jimmy Carter, Nancy Reagan, and Mother Teresa as recipients of this honor.

In 2018, in a ceremony in Washington, DC, Jim Stovall received the Lifetime Achievement in Literature Medal from the Napoleon Hill Foundation. Jim Stovall can be reached by calling 918-627-1000 or emailing Jim@JimStovall.com.

ABOUT
KRISTINE SEXTER

Kristine A. Sexter, president of WorkWise Productions and FindTrainKeep Great Employees, is an industrial and organizational consultant who has devoted more than twenty-five years to studying success and professional commitment. With an extensive background in recruiting, developing, and retaining top talent, Kristine expertly serves the manufacturing, government, healthcare, legal, and human resources industries with acclaimed results.

Leaders, managers, educators, and success-oriented people have recognized her measurably effective training and consulting programs, and she is renowned for her enthusiastic and customized strategies for creating award-winning workplace cultures.

The Oklahoma Alliance for Manufacturers has called her, *"THE authority in teaching executives and leadership teams how to find, train, and keep great employees."*

Ms. Sexter is a professional speaker, consultant, and the author of six books, including: *Rolling Out the Recognition: Employee Retention Strategies for Manufacturers.* However, she considers having coauthored this very book you are holding, *100 Worst Employees: Learning from the Very Worst How to Be Your Very Best,* with her mentor and friend, Jim Stovall, to be among the greatest honors of her professional career.

Kristine is the past president of the Oklahoma Speakers Association, was twice honored as the Speaker of the Year, and is an honors graduate of The College of New Jersey.

While born and educated on the East Coast, Kristine considers Tulsa, Oklahoma, her home—but she really misses the pizza and the ocean!

Kristine Sexter can be reached by calling 918-361-3000 or emailing Kristine@KristineSexter.com.